Unders
Guidan(

written by

Debbie Brewer

Book cover artwork by

Nikki Zalewski

ISBN: 978-0-244-78761-5

First Edition

Contents

Foreword

Dear reader,

First of all, thank you for choosing to read this book.

Spiritualism is such a grand word that widely umbrellas so many subjects.

In this book, I will be exploring the truly fascinating and growing awareness of our connection and communication with angels, but will inevitably touch upon other spiritual fields as they organically entwine, mingle and merge with each other in a manner that positively augments results.

Your decision to choose this book suggests that something about it drew you to it, or, something directed you towards it.

It may be that you are already spiritually aware and looking to build on your skills and knowledge, or want to enhance your psychic abilities. You will already be aware that what we know of spiritualism is a constantly developing phenomena. The more you learn about it, the more you realise there is in fact so much more to learn. The subject expands exponentially the deeper into it you explore. With this in mind, you will find this book a wonderful guide, with knowledge that will underline, reinforce and progress your spiritual talents, always tending towards a goal of personal enlightenment.

Perhaps you are on the path to becoming spiritually aware. If this is the case, then you should be applauded. Accepting the gift of spiritual awareness is the very first step towards personal enlightenment. For some people, acceptance is easy. They may have family or friends that already share a knowledge and belief of many spiritual ideas. For others, this acceptance can be more difficult. If you are surrounded by sceptics who may laugh or scoff, then your emerging spiritual awareness can be conflicting and confusing. If this is you, then I hold you in high respect. This was indeed me, but the call towards spiritualism was too strong and intense for me to ignore. The more I researched and read, the more drawn I was. I hope that this book serves to help you through what can feel a muddling and sometimes bewildering time as you travel on your spiritual journey. Approaching this subject with an open mind, will allow you to find this pathway an amazing, uplifting and freeing experience.

Or, maybe you are simply curious? If this is true of you, then consider that something must have stirred your curiosity enough to lead you to picking up this book. Maybe you've heard about communicating with angels and want to know more? Or maybe you are sceptical of the idea of angels, or in fact the whole idea of spiritualism as a field? I respect your doubts. Being sceptical suggests that you are a true thinker. You need some kind of proof or serious persuasion before you can agree to an idea. You cannot simply believe something you are told. You need to experience it for yourself. If this is you, then I ask that you read this book through intelligent eyes. Question everything. Doubt what you choose. But I have to ask you one thing:

If it cannot be disproved, then is it at least possible that it could be true?

Thought provoking, isn't it! My desire is that you come away from this book, having read it, with at the very least, an opened mind, and, hopefully, a new perspective on the field of spiritualism and angels.

Whatever your reason for choosing to read this book, I believe you will find this a positive experience with the answers that pertain to you as an individual, that you are looking for. And I ask the angels to guide you gently towards your own path of spiritual enlightenment.

Thank you.

What is Spirituality?

Wow, what an enormous question, with so many varied answers! Let me take the time to walk you through the idea and essence of spirituality.

First, let's look at what it is not. Spirituality is not something you can physically touch. It is not an item. Neither is it something you can scientifically prove. Although, who knows, in the future, as science progresses, there may be elements within the field of spirituality that will be proven.

Spirituality is not strictly definable. One person's idea of spirituality will be different from another's. We all approach it from our own individual perspective. Our perspectives will be tempered by our experiences and external influences, combined with our own level of psychic ability and open mindedness.

Some people appear genetically predisposed towards leading a spiritually aware life, while others will find it inexplicably hard to understand.

Some find changing their lifestyle towards one that follows a more spiritual path easy, and some will struggle, the fear of change ever present in the back of their minds.

Many people will be comfortable following a spiritually aware lifestyle, but then again, many will not. A lot of people will fear being laughed or scoffed at, and thereby choose to keep their spiritual ideals private or secret, or even deny it altogether.

Keeping your spirituality private is absolutely fine. You do not have to talk about it or display your affinity for the subject if you choose not to. Then again, you might feel an urge to connect with people of the same thought of mind. Or feel the need to explore the topic further, and expand your knowledge, through research and activity.

With all this in mind, lets revert back to our original question, what is spirituality? Now we know what it is not, we are left with the difficult task of definition.

After much research, I have found the following definitions relevant and useful, though there are hundreds more you could choose to look up.

"Spirituality is a broad concept with room for many perspectives.

It includes a sense of connection to something bigger than ourselves, and typically involves a search for the meaning of life. As such, it is a universal human experience – something that touches us all." (Krentzman, 2016)

"Spirituality is the aspect of humanity that refers to the way individuals seek and express meaning and purpose and the way they experience their connectedness to the moment, to self, to others, to nature, and to the significant or sacred." (Puchalski et al, 2009)

"Spirituality means any experience that is thought to bring the experiencer into contact with the divine (in other words, not just any experience that feels meaningful)" (Beauregard et al 2009)

"The spiritual dimension tries to be in harmony with the universe, and strives for answers about the infinite, and comes into focus when the person faces emotional stress, physical illness, or death."
(Beckman-Murray et al 1989)

Reading through these definitions, you might find one or two, or parts of them, that resonate with you. Ultimately, spiritualism is personal. You will come to know and understand your own definition, even if you are unable to put it into words or verbalise it. It is a sense, a feeling, an innate understanding on an inexplicable level. It is a unique to you. It is an infinite knowledge, with no physical presence, that you might have to accept you will never fully comprehend. There is nothing in your human language, whatever language you speak, that can properly explain it. The spiritual plane exists in a different manner, beyond our thought capability. Acceptance and faith are your tools for spiritual understanding.

"You do not need to know precisely what is happening, or exactly where it is all going. What you need is to recognize the possibilities and challenges offered by the present moment, and to embrace them with courage, faith and hope." (Thomas Merton, 1964)

Knowledge of angels can be found in written works that are many centuries old. References to them emerged originally in holy books, and the concept of angels grew as the main religions became rooted in societies across the world.

Animism

Animism is the oldest example of the human recognition of spirits that can help, hinder or hurt humankind.

It is the belief that everything has a soul or spirit, that may be good or evil, including animals, plants, rocks, mountains and stars, and that each anima has the ability to hurt, hinder or help a human.

Traditionally, each anima was a powerful spirit that had to be worshipped or feared, or attended to in some way, using spells, charms and talismans. (Got Questions Ministries, 2019).

The Victorian anthropologist, Edward Taylor, loosely defined animism as the 'belief in spirits'.

Today, modern animists see the world as full of persons, human and non-human, living together consciously, intelligently, peacefully and respectfully, the non-human element including animals, plants, mountains, metals, fire, water, wind, weather, deities, ancestors, stars, sun, etc. Animists honour the beauty and diversity of these spirits and use this relationship to nourish life and aid healing. (Foor, 2017).

Interestingly, while we hear little of animism, the majority number of people in this world are animists. The belief in nature spirits is very prevalent in Africa, Southeast Asia, rural China, Tibet, Japan, rural Central and South America, and indigenous Pacific Islands. (Eichler, 2011).

The concept of nature spirits such as those of unseen fairies, nymphs, sprites, etc, derives from animism and references to them can be found in ancient folklore across Europe, with numerous tales of spiritual assistance given to humans in distress from such creatures.

Daemons

Before the evolution of today's world's dominant religions,

daemons were believed to be spirits who would watch over people. They could be good or evil and were often linked to inanimate objects.

The term daemon is the Latin word for the Ancient Greek daimon, meaning godlike, lesser deity, and guiding spirit.

In ancient Greek mythology, daemons were considered to be divine powers, fates and guiding spirits who gave guidance and protection.

Plato, circa 400 BC, suggested, in his work, 'Symposium', that love was a daemon. He claimed that the priestess Diotima explained that "everything daemonic is between divine and mortal", with the task of daemons being "interpreting and transporting human things to the Gods and divine things to men."

In Plato's 'Apology of Socrates', Socrates claimed to have a daimonion that frequently warned in the form of a voice against mistakes that he could have made, but never actually told him what he should do. Hence, his freewill remained intact. (Susan, 2019).

Zoroastrianism

The concept of angels as we know them today is believed to have originated during the time of Zoroastrianism.

Zoroastrianism is one of the earliest religions that still remains active today, founded by the Prophet Zoroaster in ancient Iran, approximately 3500 years ago.

In Zoroastrian belief, there is a hierarchy and order of angels with names, with varying specific tasks. They are Spenta Mainyu, Amesha Spentas, Fravashis and Yazatas. They are divine energies created by the Supreme Being, Ahura Mazda, each one manifesting a beneficial blessing which Ahura Mazda has bestowed upon it, such as that of health, or right-thinking, etc.

Spenta Mainyu means Holy Creative Spirit and he is the spirit of the Supreme Being. He has dominion over humans.

Amesha Spentas are seven male and female independent spirits with individual responsibilities for residing over the physical, moral and spiritual planes. They are;

- Vohu Manah, meaning good mind, good thinking and intelligence
- Asha Vahishta, meaning truth and justice
- Khshathra Vairya , meaning righteous power
- Spenta Armaiti, meaning Holy Serenity and Devotion
- Haurvatat, meaning wholeness, integrity, health and completion
- Ameretat, meaning deathlessness and immortality

Fravashis are the holy guardian angels, and each human within Zoroastrianism is accompanied by a guardian angel throughout life to watch over them, and guard against evil spirits from whom they would need protection against.

Yazatas, or adorable ones, are spirits which assist people by protecting against evil. They each personify a different aspect within the range of ideas, virtues and nature, and some hold a higher level of importance than others. (PersianDNA, 2007).

It is often thought that Zoroastrianism provided a strong influence for Western modern religions, and they appear to be the first system of faith that introduces angels in the manner in which we believe in them today.

Emergence of the Modern Concept of Angels

In the late fifth century AD, Christian Neoplatonist, Pseudo-Dionysius the Areopagite, wrote a book called 'On the Celestial

Hierarchy'. In this work, Dionysius described the spiritual realm as having nine ranks of beings; the seraphim, cherubim, thrones, dominions, powers, authorities, principalities, archangels and angels. (Corrigan et al, 2014).

The Italian Dominican friar and priest Thomas Aquinas (1225-1274), wrote his unfinished book, 'Summa Theologica, 5 Vols'. In it, he said, "We are like children, who stand in need of masters to enlighten us and direct us; God has provided for this, by appointing his angels to be our teachers and guides... Angels transcend every religion, every philosophy, every creed. In fact, angels have no religion as we know it... Their existence precedes every religious system that has ever existed on Earth." (Aquinas, 1270).

Thomas Aquinas classified the angels into three spheres, also referred to as hierarchies or triads. Within each sphere are three angelic choirs, also referred to as orders of angels, resulting in nine choirs altogether.

The hierarchy in which Thomas Aquinas classed the angels, was built on the founding ideas of Pseudo-Dionysius the Areopagite, and is still in use today.

We will go on to discuss the modern idea of angel hierarchy later in this book.

Angel therapy is a non-denominational spiritual healing method, involving working with angels to assist and heal in all aspects of daily life.

It is thought to be a form of psychological counselling that integrates traditional counselling techniques with a belief in the reality of angels. (Encyclopedia.com, 2019)

It is based on the concept that believing in angels and thereby becoming aware of them, enables us to communicate with them, and ask for healing, inspiration, protection and guidance towards leading a happy and fulfilled life.

Angel healing therapy is known to assist in all aspects of health, both physical and mental, emotional and spiritual.

Angel therapy can be used to provide peace and balance in life, when faced with turmoil and confusion. Similarly, it can also be used in more direct issues. Whatever you need help with, the angels can assist you.

For example, they can

- Help with decision making
- Elevate your consciousness on a spiritual journey
- Heal emotional hurts, jealously and the pain of grief
- Find lost objects
- Get a job
- Heal physically after an accident or illness
- Protect your home

- Protect your family and loved ones
- Be forgiving
- Find joy in life

In fact, the list can go on. Angels can assist with anything you ask, provided it is for good.

Angels do not acknowledge any kind of human hierarchy. They do not distinguish people by race, religion, age, or status. You do not have to be leading a devout or religious life. Anyone, whoever you are, can ask for help and the angels will respond. They reside in the spiritual realm specifically to aid mankind.

You can ask for help from an angel at any time. They are always there, and always ready to support and help you. You can also ask for help for someone else, such as protection for a family member or friend.

Angel therapy can help people connect with relevant angels, ones that are most likely to be able to help with a specific issue at hand. It can also help people get to know their guardian angel.

When you come to realise and accept angels into your life, and actively practice asking for help and guidance, you will find that whatever your circumstance, life will become easier and you will feel happier.

Psychic Ability

It is commonly thought that humans do not use the full potential of their brain cells, an idea suggested by American psychologist William James, who said, "We are making use of only a small part of our possible mental and physical resources." (James, 1914). This would imply that there are further abilities and skills that humans are capable of, but which most do not recognise or utilise.

Everyone has a degree of psychic ability, whether they know it or not. Some are aware of it and accept it, others choose to deny it.

For example, have you ever experienced the phone ringing, and when you check, it is the same

31

person as you were thinking about that very moment? This is your psychic ability kicking in.

Have you ever experienced deja-vu, the feeling that you have been in a situation or place before, even though you know you've never been there? Again, this is evidence of your psychic ability.

Have you ever had a good or bad 'gut-feeling' about someone or something, an instinct about a situation? How many times have you been told to follow or believe in your intuition?

Gut-feelings and intuition are non-measurable intangible phenomenon, impossible to prove and difficult to explain. They are involuntary reactions that have no logical rationale. Yet we all have these abilities. These are your psychic abilities, based on insight and perception. This is your sixth sense, after the five senses of sight, sound, smell, touch and taste.

Angels will use our psychic abilities and spiritual gifts to connect with us on a spiritual level. Becoming aware and working to improve these will enable you to learn to communicate and understand angel communications more clearly and effectively.

Spiritual Gifts

Within the field of psychic ability, we have spiritual gifts of varying types and to varying levels and these fall into eight categories.

- Clairvoyance
- Clairaudience
- Clairgustance

- Clairsentience
- Clairalience
- Clairempathy
- Clairtangency
- Claircognizance

These are talents which allow you to connect with the spirit world, including communication with angels and other spirits.

If you allow yourself to open up and receive messages from your sixth sense, and practice your ability, you may find that you have a stronger talent in one category, more than another. You simply have to recognise you have sensed a form of communication in your consciousness that did not come through the usual five senses of see, hear, taste, touch or smell.

Clairvoyance

Clairvoyance is the most common spiritual gift and it literally means clear seeing.

A clairvoyant is someone who receives intuitive information visually. Some people will refer to this as third eye visions or second sight, or seeing something in the mind's eye. What they see will often be symbolic of a person, situation or event of the past, present, and less commonly, the future. (Lee, 2012).

The visual information a clairvoyant might see, may arrive as visions, pictures or symbols. It may be like a snapshot image in your mind, or a vision of a symbol that represents something specific such as a date, person, event or situation, or a moving picture in your head.

You may have already had clairvoyant events, and not really taken notice of them.

- Have you ever noticed flashes, shimmers or sparkly light out of the corner of your eye?
- Have to ever been disturbed by movement in your peripheral vision when there is no movement in the room?
- Have you experienced an image randomly flash spontaneously before your eyes, or in your mind, with no apparent reason or connection to what you are currently thinking or doing?

- Have you ever noticed ethereal colours surrounding a person or living thing? ie, their aura?
- Have you experienced dreams that have been so vivid that they seemed very real.

These clairvoyant connections are not visible or tangible in our earthly world, and no two clairvoyants will see the same image or vision. (Lee, 2019)

Using clairvoyance, you can receive messages and hints from the spirit or angel world. These messages may be light and clear, or cloudy, blurry and indistinct. They may be obvious, and easy to understand, or difficult to decipher. But even the less distinct and comprehensive messages will eventually become clear with time as their meanings become apparent with events of the future.

Being Fey

Connected with clairvoyance is the ability of being 'fey'. To be fey, is to see ahead. It is an old Gaelic word that means to be able to see what is about to happen using supernatural powers of clairvoyance.

The dictionary definition of 'fey', is 'giving an impression of vague unworldliness or mystery, and having supernatural powers of clairvoyance. (English Oxford Living Dictionary, 2019).

"Have you ever met someone who speaks like they're casting spells and has a distant look in their eyes? That's a fey person, someone who seems like they come from another world... supernatural in a vague way." (Vocabulary.com Dictionary, nd).

Someone who is fey, is typically shy, with an unearthly mystical quality. They are said to be enchanted with whimsical fairy like similarities with unconventional powers enabling them to see near and distant future events.

Developing Your Clairvoyance to Communicate with Angels

Like all skills, belief in yourself and practice will enable you to develop your clairvoyant ability. There are several exercises to help with this.

Auras

One exercise to help you develop your clairvoyance is to learn to see auras.

Auras are the strongest visual concept in the spirit world that you can tap into. They surround all living things and will linger in angels when they are near.

An aura is an energy field that surrounds and encompasses every being. It can be any colour, it can have more than one colour, and it's colour can change and vary. It can also be bright or dull, shiny or flat. It is an energy that we radiate, a vibe.

"An aura is your life force energy field around you. I see it in colour. We all have our own inherent combination. It's like a snowflake." – Mystic Michaela, aura reader.

These auras may appear layered, or splotchy like, and each colour holds a specific representation. You will have one or two inherent colours that are specific to you and your inner soul, and these colours maybe be altered or affected by your emotional or physical state. (Estrada, 2018)

How To See An Aura

- Sit quietly, facing someone else a few feet away from you and sitting at the same level as you.
- Make sure the room is quiet and calm and free from interruption.
- Be sitting comfortably, with the temperature of the room being right for

you, so that you can relax and focus.

- Focus on your breathing. Breathe slowly for a few moments.
- Now stare at the person opposite you. Stare at their central chest area. Do not focus on them. Focus *through* them. Let your eyesight relax through them.
- Allow your peripheral vision to permeate into your field of vision. You will start to see colour around the person in front of you. It may be thin to start with, but as your clairvoyant ability increases, the colour may become thicker, brighter or more vivid.

Aura Colour Meanings

The aura around each person will have at least one colour, and will be prone to altering according to the physical and emotional state of the individual. Just by reading and understanding a person's aura, they can be helped, by learning what areas of their lives are dominant and influencing them, and whether they are on a path that is authentic to them.

The brightness of an aura also has indications. For example, if a person is feeling confident and comfortable, their aura will be shining brightly. But a person who is feeling insecure may have a weaker or duller aura. A very strong consuming emotion within the individual will manifest a strong aura.

Yellow

A person with a naturally yellow aura is inquisitive, busy and curious. They're overall feeling will be that of happiness. They have intellect, logic and creativity, but they can be irresponsible and unstable. Yellow is a colour of health, balance, vitality, lightness, humour and humility.

Strength of colour:

- A pale yellow aura will signify an introverted state.
- A primrose yellow aura will signify a cheerful state
- A lemon yellow aura will signify a strong-willed state
- A buttercup yellow aura will signify a highly focused state

- A golden yellow aura will signify an inspirational state.

Green

A naturally green aura surrounding a person indicates compassion and feminine wisdom and intelligence. They are inherently kind, and of a healing nature, but can be prone to envy, jealousy and guilt. Green is a colour of family, support and strength, harmony, love and communication.

Strength of colour:

- A pale green aura will signify a leaning towards a spiritual state.
- An apple green aura will signify a healing state.

- An iridescent green aura will signify a sociable state.
- An emerald green aura will signify a problem solving state.
- A jade green aura will signify a compassionate state.
- A turquoise green aura will signify a state of tough resolve.

Purple

A person with a purple aura surrounding them will tend to be emotional, intuitive, creative and artistic. They can be soothing, calm spiritual people, though still ambitious with a taste for luxury. They can sometimes have carry an air of mystery and moodiness. They are temperate, appreciative and gracious in nature and have a certain connectiveness to the universe as a whole.

Strength of colour:

- A lilac aura will signify a spiritually stable state.
- A magenta aura will signify an entrepreneurial state.
- A mauve aura will signify a modest lifestyle state.
- A violet aura will signify a state of humility.
- A dark brown aura will signify a strong level of underlying common sense.

Red

A person displaying a red aura will tend to be strong and assertive, enjoying risk and winning ambitions and they will embrace fame. They are naturally focused more on the earthly realm. They possess clarity, integrity and charity, and have a powerful energy for passion, love and strength. They will have tendencies towards anger and danger, but will be grounded, have stamina, and will enjoy spontaneity.

Strength of colour:

- A crimson aura will signify a multi-talented state.
- A vermillion aura will signify an extremely creative state.
- A claret aura will signify a tenacious state.
- A scarlet aura will signify a confident state.

- A rustic aura will signify a highly volatile state.

Blue

Unlike people with red auras, those with blue auras do not like being the centre of attention. They are selfless healers, who tend to have empathic abilities, capable of absorbing and feeling other people's emotions as their own. They possess an air of inner knowledge and a constant search for self-improvement. They will have a need for stillness, introspection and security and will be naturally tranquil, loyal, intelligent and peaceful.

Strength of colour:

- An aqua aura will signify a healing state.

- A pale blue aura will signify a highly sensitive state.
- A sky blue aura will signify a highly instinctive state.
- A cobalt blue aura will signify a highly intuitive state.
- A royal blue aura will signify a state of satisfaction and acceptance.
- A navy blue aura will signify a safe and secure state.
- An indigo aura will signify a state of psychic talent.

Orange

People with sunset coloured auras tend to be creative and fun loving. They enjoy a sense of togetherness. They are diligent people with courage and confidence and an ever present air of friendliness. They can suffer from ignorance and sluggishness, but can also be enthusiastic and optimistic, free and extrovert.

Strength of colour:

- An apricot aura will signify a communicative state.
- An orange aura will signify a motivated state.
- A pumpkin orange aura will signify a disciplined state.
- An amber aura will signify a courageous state.
- A caramel aura will signify a state of occupational change.

Other Colours

Less common colours can occur in auras which also have meanings:

- A pale pink aura will signify a true love state.
- A salmon pink aura will signify a state of true vocation.
- A faun aura will signify an end to life problems.
- A chocolate brown aura will signify a state of being in tune with the environment.
- A russet brown aura will signify a hard working state.
- A terracotta aura will signify an unconventional state.
- A silver grey aura will signify a calm spiritual state.

- A silver aura will signify a very spiritual state.
- A white aura will signify a highly tuned state.
- A cream aura will signify a state of being on the right path.
- A pearl aura will signify a state of being in tune with the spiritual world
- A zinc aura will signify a sexualised state.

As you go about your day, you can use this new skill. You can casually notice the people around you and their auras. By relaxing and staring at living things and focusing through them rather than at them, you can become aware, not only of their auras, but of movement in your peripheral vision and in time, you will start to see images of angels.

Zener Cards

Another way to develop your clairvoyance is through the use of Zener cards.

Zener cards were created to test the theory of extra sensory perception, or ESP for short, by perceptual psychologist Karl Zener and parapsychologist J. B. Rhine, at Duke University in the 1930s.

They developed an experiment whereby cards would be held up in front of a subject, who was then asked to guess what was on the card. The percentage of correct answers would then be recorded and used to determine whether the subject had ESP.

They began the experiment using regular playing cards but soon abandoned these due to there being too many combinations. So instead, Zener and Rhine developed a set of five cards, each with a simple design. These five designs were the hollowed ring, the hollowed rectangle, the Greek cross, the hollowed five pointed star and three vertical wavy lines.

Zener Cards

Zener and Rhine concluded that any subject who identified more than 20% of the cards correctly must be influenced by something other than chance, namely the possession of the skill of ESP. (Schultz, 2011).

Today, each modern day pack of Zener cards contains twenty five cards, with five cards of each shape drawn on a white background.

Practice with Zener Cards

To practice, you should sit with a partner, facing each other in silence. Make sure you are relaxed and the ambience of the room is calm. Your partner can hold up a card with the back of it to you and you must concentrate on the card.

After a while, the shape of the card will come to you in your mind's eye, and you should say what you think it is out loud. Your partner should place the card face down on the table in two piles, those you guessed correctly, and those you guessed wrong, and then repeat the process until all the cards have been used.

At the end, count up how many you got right and how many you got wrong. The odds of you getting 20% correct through simple guessing is the base line statistic.

If you have got more than 20% correct, then you are evolving your clairvoyance. If you got less, then you need to practice.

You will find, as with any skill, with daily practice, you will be able to improve your score and hence, your skill of clairvoyance.

Clairaudience

Clairaudience is the second most common spiritual gift and it literally means clear hearing.

It is the ability to hear things from the spirit and angel realm that are not picked up by your natural range and which may not be audible to other people. It is often referred to as the little voice in your head, and may come to you in the form of words, whispers, phrases, sounds such as bells, chimes or tinkles, or music.

These communications can seem to almost appear in your head and may be something your guardian angel or another angel is trying to tell you.

People with a natural flair for clairaudience tend to exhibit the following traits:

- They habitually talk to themselves when alone.
- They learn best through the mode of listening rather than by reading, writing or kinaesthetically.
- They dislike sudden or loud noises.
- They crave peace and quiet and alone time
- They can suffer from regular headaches
- They can hear whispering or talking in the distance when they are alone.
- They can recognise a message sent specifically for them through the TV or radio.
- They can 'feel' music and be spiritually moved by it.
- They can hear advice from voices in their mind.

- They may hear some uncanny noise such as a hum, associated with specific structures or buildings, that resonates with only them, that no one else can hear.

(Davies, 2017).

Developing Your Clairaudience to Communicate with Angels

To develop your clairaudience, sit quietly alone, in a calm room with an ambient temperature, and close your eyes. Listen carefully and deliberately hear what is around you. Accept what you hear. It may be a background noise of birds chirping or traffic noise that you would not normally notice or pay any attention to. Hear your breathing as you inhale and exhale.

Take your time. Relax. This is your relaxed state. Now listen deeper. Listen for other sounds such as sighs, and noises that are not part of the normal background buzz. This is your skill of clairaudience. Keep listening.

If you practice clairaudience on a daily basis, you will learn to recognise other sounds and words that can only be heard while you are listening at this deeper level, tapping into the sounds of the spirit and angel realm. Angels will want to connect with you and will communicate with you.

Heating words from the angel realm will begin slowly and gradually. For example, you may hear the word 'stop', when someone is lying to you, or something is not right about them. Or their words may not coincide with their intentions, so you may hear a second internal dialogue running through your mind.

With practice, you will learn the ability to tune out to the noise of every day whenever you choose and tune in to any communications from your angels.

Clairgustance and Clairalience

Clairgustance and clairalience are less common spiritual gifts.

Clairgustance

Clairgustance literally means clear tasting. It is the ability to understand a message from the spirit and angel realm through tasting something, without putting anything in your mouth.

Clairalience

Clairalience means clear smelling and it is the ability to understand a message from the spirit and angel realm through smelling something that isn't there. It might be just a slight whiff that will bring forth a memory or suggest a place, person, situation or event.

Developing Your Clairgustance and Clairalience to Communicate with Angels

To develop these abilities, start by trying to get as much variety of different things to smell and taste. With each smell or taste, take your time to savour the flavour and think about all the flavours and smells that make up each individual ingredient of what you are eating or smelling. Try closing your eyes so that you can focus more directly on what you are tasting or smelling without being affected by your other senses.

You are teaching your sense of smell and taste to recognise differences and you are building a repertoire of smells and tastes.

Each time you do this, your sense of smell and taste will become more sensitive and more capable of recognising and distinguishing between certain smells and tastes and you will become more discerning and able to specifically identify their individual derivatives.

You can further fine tune these senses by asking a partner to offer you different foods while you have a blindfold on. Try similar foods and learn the difference. Eg, learn the different taste and smell of an apple and a pear, or a tangerine and a satsuma, or cinnamon and nutmeg.

Next, sit in a quiet calm room, close your eyes, and imagine eating and smelling different foods, one at a time. If your senses are finely tuned, you may invoke a physical response. For example, if you imagine eating an orange, your mouth might start watering, and you might actually feel like you can taste it, even though it is not there.

Now you can try phoning a friend and ask them to eat or drink something without telling you what it is. Take a few minutes, close your eyes and relax, and see if you can start to taste or smell what it is they are having.

If you practice, you will inevitably sharpen your clairgustance and clairalience and soon you will recognise an unexpected smell or taste that does not relate to anything on the physical plane, but which may be a message from an angel, maybe your guardian angel, as a form of communication to guide you towards a certain path. This smell or taste will have a connection with something specific to you, and it will have meaning that you will be able to decipher. (Smith, 2018)

Clairsentience, Clairempathy, Clairtangency and Claircognizance

Clairsentience, Clairempathy, Clairtangency and claircognizance are also less common spiritual gifts.

Clairsentience

Clairsentience literally means clear feeling. It is the ability to understand a message from the spirit and angel realm through an irrational physical feeling about something, such as experiencing an emotion with no apparent trigger. It might be a gut feeling, or the unnerving feeling that something just isn't right. It might be a feeling about a person, or about a place or building or object. Something connected invokes the physical response in the clairsentient.

Clairempathy

Clairempathy means clear emotional feeling, and is the ability to sense another being's thoughts, emotions, reactions and symptoms. Unlike a clairsentient, you do not actually feel it, you simply inexplicably become aware of it. For example, being able to sense an atmosphere in a room where two people are sitting. Maybe they have had an argument. But you did not know that, you just sensed it. This is your clairempathy.

Clairtangency

Clairtangency means clear touching. It is the ability to receive and understand messages through contact or close proximity with another person or object. For example, holding a watch may give you insights into the owner of that watch. Touching an old building may allow you to understand a former event that may have happened there. Holding a person's hand could allow you a perception of something in their world, otherwise unknown.

Claircognizance

Claircognizance means clear knowing and it is the ability to understand a message from the spirit and angel realm because you just inexplicably suddenly know something. It can be called intuitive thought. Because it is a definite knowledge, it is unlikely to be open to misinterpretation. It is a strong clear guidance. When you have a claircognizant episode, recognise it, accept it and act on it immediately. The more you react in this manner, the more obvious these moments will be when they come to you. (Pavlina, 2010).)

Acceptance

Accepting these spiritual gifts into your life will allow you further avenues of communication with angels. You should always be thankful for your gifts and abilities and use them often. These are natural gifts of communication which can enhance both your life and the lives of others, and with practice, you will be able to strengthen your ability to connect with the angels and use these gifts with confidence.

Indigo, Crystal and Rainbow Children

Indigo, Crystal and Rainbow children are often referred to as the Star Children. They are born within specific time frames and have heightened spiritual abilities, enabling them to detect, communicate and understand angels more clearly and accurately. When they are born, they maintain more of their spiritual connection to the Divine.

These children have the ability to awaken human consciousness towards truth and light. It is said that their purpose is to "progress the ascension of humanity", and that they do this through "love, manifestation, integrity, peace and cooperation". (Beckler, 2014).

The Star Children have elevated levels of psychic, telepathic and empathic abilities, and are able to embrace and further spiritual teachings. Because of their special purpose, to enable and elevate human evolvement, they are very well protected by the angels.

Indigo Children

Indigo children are called this because their auras are a clear indigo in colour. People with this colour aura tend to be spiritually highly evolved.

These children were among those born from around the 1970s onwards. They are typically intelligent, excitable and lack concentration when bored.

They can be rebellious and questioning of authority, often hyperactive, and will not be controlled. They will not conform unless they are allowed free will and their respect is earnt.

They free us from past limitations and challenge old beliefs, making the way for new ideas and growth.

Crystal Children

Crystal children were born from the late 1990s onwards. They tend to have large penetrating eyes and crystal-like twinkly auras. They are calm, kind and warm hearted. They are also compassionate, enlightened and radiate love. They have a connection with the earthly world drawing them to animals and nature and they have heightened levels of sensitivity and empathic ability.

These children have the power to awake a universal consciousness to promote peace and oneness and bring forth a safe and more secure world.

Rainbow Children

Rainbow children are the most recent of these higher spiritually evolved children to be born. They are very psychic and their clairvoyance and clairaudience comes easily and naturally to them.

These children radiate a rainbow aura and energy of unconditional love. Often the children of the crystal generation before, they are fearless and giving in nature.

Because of their loving nature, they are unaffected by negative emotions. They can often appear to be living in their own world and be unreactive. But they are more highly evolved spiritually than any other human, and they show us the potential we have for understanding pure love and light.

Not all angels are created equal. Also some have specific roles and designations. (Castro, 2017).

As previously explained, It was Zoroastrianism who provided the first system of faith that introduced angels in the manner in which we believe in them today.

Then Pseudo-Dionysius the Areopagite of the fifth century AD suggested the angel realm was divided into nine hierarchical ranks.

It was the Italian Dominican friar and priest Thomas Aquinas (1225-1274) who classified the angels into three broad spheres, also referred to as hierarchies or triads. Within each sphere are three angelic choirs, also referred to as orders of angels, resulting in nine choirs altogether.

It is this hierarchical structure that we still use today.

According to their placement on this hierarchy, those angels above have more power than those further down. The angels at the top are closest to God, and so have the most power. Angels which are lower in the hierarchy, such as the archangels and the regular angels, are the ones to which we typically have access.

First Hierarchy: First Sphere (First Triad)

First Choir (Order)

Seraphim

Second Choir (Order)

Cherubim

Third Choir (Order)

Thrones (also called Orphanim or Galgallin or Wheels or Many Eyed Ones or God-bearing)

Middle Hierarchy: Second Sphere (Second Triad)

First Choir (Order)

Dominions (Dominations) (also called Lordships or Kuoriotes)

Second Choir (Order)

Virtues (also called Strongholds)

Third Choir (Order)

Powers (also called Authorities)

Third Hierarchy: Third Sphere (Third Triad)

First Choir (Order)

Principalities (Principals) (also called Rulers)

Second Choir (Order)

Archangels

Third Choir (Order)

Angels (also called regular angels)

Hierarchy Summary

God

Seraphim

Cherubim

Thrones

Dominions

Virtues

Powers

Principalities

Archangels

Angels

Man

Angels within the first sphere are the closest to God. They have the most power and serve him directly. They can be referred to as the heavenly servants. The angels within the first sphere are the only ones who can see and adore God directly.

Seraphim

Seraphim literally means 'burning one' and are seen as if they seem to be on fire or burning and radiating pure light. They are said to be aflame with love for God.

These are the highest angelic class. Their task is tending to God's throne and remaining closest to him at all times, always showering him with praise.

Seraphim have three pairs of wings. One pair to fly, one pair to conceal their face, and one pair to cover their feet in respect.

Technically, they are so divine that they do not actually possess the status of angel. More, they are a division of the holy messenger. (Castro, 2017).

Archangels, with a capital 'A' are the highest of the seraphim, and this is where Archangel Michael sits. These are not to be confused with archangels, with a lowercase 'a'. We will discuss the Archangels in a later chapter.

Cherubim

The word cherubim can mean a beautiful innocent looking child, often depicted in art with small wings and also often referred to as a cherub. However, these are actually Putti, only the word Putti has long been forgotten and replaced by cherubim. They should not be confused with a cherubim angel.

Cherubim, as a word, actually means 'fullness of wisdom'. Cherubim angels have four faces representing the four elements. They have the face of a lion for fire, an eagle for air, a bull for earth, and a man for water. They have a lions body, four conjoined wings covered with eyes, with human hands under their wings, and four oxen feet. Their appearance is said to be quite terrifying.

They are radiant, powerful, majestic creatures, and they surround God's throne, guarding the way to the throne, procuring the creator's bidding and protecting him. They were sent to guard the gates of Eden after man was driven out, and to guard the way to the tree of life.

They shine with the light of the knowledge of God, the knowledge of the mysteries of God and the depth of his wisdom. They are enlightened and are capable of enlightening others.

These are the most mentioned of all the angels in the Christian bible.

Thomas Aquinas believed that Satan (also called Lucifer) was a Cherubim before he fell and became the head of the fallen angels.

Thrones, also known as Orphanim, Galgallin, Wheels, Many Eyed Ones and God-bearing.

Throne angels are creatures who are tasked with being the actual chariots of God, driven by the Cherubim. They are said to be great fiery wheels that sparkle like brass, containing many eyes. They reside in the area of the cosmos where material form begins to take shape. It is said that God rests upon them and they are forever in his presence. (Guiley, 1996).

The throne angels are symbols of authority, the elders, carrying the throne of God. They are able to mete out God's justice, continually contemplating it, and carry out his decisions. They listen to the will of

God and present our human prayers to him.

The throne angels can convey messages from the essence of God's word to the lower classes of angels, who can then, in turn, pass them on to humans.

Angels classed within the second sphere of the hierarchy are the administers of creation. They are heavenly governors guiding and ruling the lower angels and subjecting matter to God's will.

Dominions (Dominations), also known as Lordships and Kuoriotes

The dominion angels regulate the duties of the lower angels, keep them in line, and ensure that God's wishes communicated to them from the first sphere are carried out.

They are considered to resemble beautiful humans. They have one pair of magnificent wings and carry an orb of bright light on the head of their sceptre or the pommel of their sword.

The dominion angels are considered to be free and serve God voluntarily and unceasingly, with joy.

Very rarely, dominions reveal themselves to humans.

Virtues, also known as Strongholds

The virtue angels are the angels of grace and the source of virtue. There is an abundance of virtue for all and it flows from the virtue angels to angels below on the hierarchy and to humans below them.

These angels carry out God's blessings to the Earth in the form of miracles and heavenly signs, such as healing sickness and foretelling the future.

They are often referred to as the 'brilliant' or 'shining' ones and are virile and unshakeable in doing God's will. They are the hardest workers of all the angels.

The virtue angels are also tasked with maintaining the physical laws of the universe, according to the will of God.

Powers, also known as Authorities

The power angels are the warriors of the angelic realm. They are the bearers of consciousness and oppose evil, and they are the keepers of history and time.

They appear as soldiers wearing armour, and carry shields, spears and chains used to restrain the power of the devil and evil spirits and demons for eternity. As such, they are tasked with preventing the fallen angels from causing harm.

They maintain the creative energy flowing within the universe and the cosmos, keeping them in predictable balance.

The third sphere of angels act as messengers for humans. They are concerned with heavenly guidance and protection. They remain pure, wise and powerful, but are the farthest from God in the angel hierarchy.

Principalities (Principals), also known as Rulers

The principal angels guide, manage and protect cities, nations, races, rulers, and large groups of people and institutions that come together in God's name. They carry out tasks delegated to them by higher dominion angels and in turn manage bands of angels and task them with fulfilling divine orders.

Principal angels wear a crown and carry a sceptre. They can bestow blessings to the human world and are the educators and guardians of humans against harm from evil. They inspire and ignite creativity in art and science in humans and can raise worthy people to higher offices in the human world.

Archangels

The archangels, with a lowercase 'a', are the guardian angels of nations and countries. They are given the distinction 'arch', which means 'ruling' to signify their status above the common angel. Archangels with a capital 'A' are the highest of the seraphim in the first sphere, and should not be confused, This is the difference between archangels and Archangels.

They carry God's most important messages to humans, heralding and announcing all great and glorious news. They reveal prophecies, knowledge, and help humans understand God's will.

The archangels are also the creators of miracles on behalf of mankind and can visit humans when their presence is asked for.

They are the rulers of the regular angels, protecting humans from evil and relaying divine messages.

Angels

These angels are the regular angels and there are legions upon legions upon legions of them, still pure, wise and powerful, but the farthest from God and the closest to humans.

Their duties include listening for us to call upon them for help with specific tasks. They serve humanity, guarding us from harm, guiding us and imparting wisdom. They never leave us, even when we have done wrong and are always available to help. We just have to want help and ask for it.

These angels are the most capable at communicating with us on our level and in a manner that our human minds can understand.

Guardian angels reside among the regular angels in the third sphere and we will discuss guardian angels in more detail later.

The Seven Principle Archangels

There are seven principle Archangels who are always ready, willing and able to connect with you when you ask. They each have individual responsibilities and associations, which often overlap.

These Archangels are thought to have been regular archangels, until a war broke out in heaven, when Satan (Lucifer) believed he was God's equal and he and his angel followers rebelled. As they fought, these seven archangels positioned themselves between God and Satan, protecting God, and so God elevated them to reside with him among the seraphim. Satan and his angels were cast out of heaven and became the fallen angels of the underworld.

Book of Revelation, 12:7-10,

7 Then war broke out in heaven. Michael and his angels fought against the dragon, and the dragon and his angels fought back.

8 But he was not strong enough, and they lost their place in heaven.

9 The great dragon was hurled down – that ancient serpent called the devil, or Satan, who leads the whole world astray. He was hurled to the earth, and his angels with him.

The Archangel's names always end in 'el' which means 'in God'. They are:

- Michael
- Gabriel

- Raphael
- Chamuel
- Jophiel
- Uriel
- Zadkiel

These seven angels stand before God, in his presence, possessing great power and spiritual authority. They each have many varied associations which people can refer to and use when deciding which Archangel they wish to connect with.

Archangel Michael

The name 'Michael' means 'he who is as God' or 'like unto God'.

Archangel Michael is the highest angel of protection and the leader and most powerful of all the angels. He is said to sit with the seraphim nearest to God and his powers are derived from the will of God.

He is often depicted as muscular and athletic, with intense facial expressions and powerful body language. He wears armour and holds his sword of sapphire, emblazoned by a blue flame, poised over a pinned down demon, symbolising his purpose of slaying ego and fear, through courage, strength and protection. Sometimes he is depicted as carrying the scales of divine justice.

Archangel Michael is a protector of humans and their belongings. As the warrior of heaven, he will fight for truth and what is right for you. He works continuously, fighting the forces of darkness to bring peace and harmony to all.

He is the protector of the innocent through miraculous intervention and offers his courage, power and strength for all who ask, defending and bringing forth integrity, truth and love.

He protects humans from real and imaginary fears, helping us achieve our ambitions and goals. He will assist us in working through darkness into light, and in releasing fear with courage and bravery.

He can fix broken emotions, such as hearts and relationships, releasing fear and doubt, invoking clarity of thought and providing support in making life changes.

He is considered to be the angel of justice, righteousness and mercy, upholding the law and law making, and supports personal leadership and life purpose aspirations.

As the warrior, he supports all military troops and fighters who are just and in the right. He is also concerned with socio politics and the work of the common man.

He can help with lack of motivation and incentive and brings patience and perseverance. He shields us from negative energy when we are trying to cope with troubles or challenges.

Associations:

- Virtue: Charity and self-sacrifice
- Aura Colour: Purple, Royal Blue and Gold
- Scents: Chamomile, Frankincense, Rosemary and Sage
- Day of the week: Sunday, the first day

- Symbol: Hexagram
- Season: Summer
- Direction: South
- Metal: Gold and Brass
- Zodiac: Leo, Sagittarius and Aries
- Planet: Venus and the Sun
- Element: Fire
- Chakra: Throat chakra
- Crystal: Sugulite, Amber, Golden Topaz, Clear Quartz
- Tarot Card: The Judgement Card

Archangel Gabriel

The name 'Gabriel' means 'God is mighty', or 'messenger of God'.

Archangel Gabriel is thought to be a female Archangel, also referred to as the angel of revelation. She is known for announcing the immaculate conception to Mary, and the births of John the Baptist and Jesus Christ.

Luke, 1:26-28

...the angel Gabriel was sent by God to city of Galilee named Nazareth, to a virgin betrothed to a man whose name was Joseph, of the house of David. The virgin's name was Mary.

Archangel Gabriel is usually depicted with long golden hair and flowing white robes and she is holding a copper trumpet, symbolising announcement.

Considered to be the profound messenger of the Divine, the messenger of heaven, Archangel

Gabriel's primary role is to deliver powerful messages of love, grace, wisdom and guidance, to those who need and ask for assistance.

She assists with communications and messages through the spoken and written word, supporting writers, journalists, teachers and parents to find motivation, confidence and clarity in their work.

She provides spiritual guidance through dreams and visions helping us to know what we should do and which path to follow in our lives, through self-nurturing and self-love.

Archangel Gabriel helps with purification and being born again, new beginnings and the birth of new ideas. She can assist parents with fertility problems, those who need help conceiving, pregnancy, childbirth, adopting or raising children.

She supports and provides inspiration to those who work in the fields of communication, marketing, secretarial, hospitality, travel and tourism, education and the arts and crafts, and will help humans find their vocations.

She can assist in conflict resolution, and will help humans to overcome fear and procrastination in communication.

Associations:

- Virtue: Diligence
- Aura Colour: White and Silver
- Scents: Jasmine, Rose, Eucalyptus and Myrrh

- Day of the week: Wednesday
- Season: Winter
- Direction: West
- Symbol: Nine Pointed Star
- Metal: Silver
- Zodiac: Pisces, Cancer and Scorpio
- Planet: Saturn and the Moon
- Element: Water
- Chakra: Sacral Chakra
- Crystal: Moonstone, Aquamarine, Pearls and Selenite
- Tarot Card: The Temperance Card

Archangel Raphael

The name 'Raphael' means 'the healing of God' or 'God heals'.

He is the angel of physical, mental, spiritual and emotional healing and is associated with divine love. We can ask Archangel Raphael for help when we need to heal ourselves and our children from all types of sickness, disease and illnesses. We can also ask for help when we want to heal others. He is also known for his powerful depth of kindness.

Tobit 3:17

And Raphael was sent to heal them both, that is, to scale away the whiteness of Tobit's eyes.

Tobit 12:15

I am Raphael, one of the seven holy angels, which represent the prayers of the saints, and which go in and out before the glory of the Holy One.

We can also ask him to heal pets, wildlife and livestock.

His healing powers do not just relate to the physical body. He can also heal matters related to the mind and spirit. He helps clear away any stress or fear that can be affecting health and inspires us to make healthy lifestyle choices. He leads us towards a positive outlook consisting of hope, levity and laughter, no matter how grave our situation might be.

Also, known as the "Medicine of God', he can be called on to heal broken relationships, difficult situations, unwanted addictions and cravings, and memory improvement. He is good for meditation and calm breathing when in hospices or hospitals, for healing the sick, ill and injured or to help guide us through the pain of bereavement and grief. He will assist us when we are facing surgery or illness, both slight or serious, and help us heal after.

As the patron of the sick, he supports all health care workers, especially nurses, doctors, faith healers and pharmacists.

Archangel Raphael is also the patron of travellers and he supports those who work in the transportation industry. He guides us when we are away from home on journeys near or far, keeping us safe, especially when travelling by air.

He is tasked with assisting in restoring and maintaining harmony and peace among mankind. He is the guardian of weddings and conjugal love.

Archangel Raphael is known to communicate through our intuitions, thoughts, dreams and ideas and by simply answering our calls for medical intervention through the action of healing.

As the embodiment of compassion, he is often depicted as having a bright glowing green light emanating from him and surrounding him. In one hand he carries a staff with a caduceus upon it, which is the ancient symbol of the medical arts, or a walking stick. In the other hand he carries a bowl of healing balm or a medicine jar.

Caduceus

The caduceus is an ancient symbol of the medical arts and it consists of two snakes winding around a winged staff.

Associations:

- Virtue: Humility
- Aura Colour: Yellow and Green
- Scents: Lavender, Lily of the Valley, Mint, Bergamot and Thyme
- Day of the week: Thursday
- Season: Spring
- Direction: East and North
- Zodiac: Aquarius, Libra and Gemini
- Metal: Quicksilver and Aluminium
- Planet: Mercury and Mars
- Symbol: Eight Pointed Star
- Element: Air
- Chakra: Heart
- Crystal: Emerald, Malachite, Jade, Citrine, Aventurine and Yellow Calcite

- Tarot Card: The Lovers Card

Archangel Chamuel

The name 'Chamuel' means 'Seeker of God' or 'he who sees God' and she is the Archangel of peace and divine justice.

Archangels Chamuel judges and determines good and evil. She is tasked with bringing peace and harmony to the world, protecting the world from fear and alleviating tension.

She is said to be all knowing and sees the interconnectedness between all things. She is the angel of peaceful relationships between all things, and the angel of courage and adoration.

She can build or repair relationships. She can bring together people who we need to augment our lives, whether for business, socially, or intimately. She will assist in finding new love, seeking the love of our children, and mending rifts among families.

She will assist the lonely, by finding them companionship.

She will help us find strength and courage when we feel we have none left, to enable us to overcome any kind of adversity, anxiety or despair. She will assist us in finding time for ourselves and self-love and self-acceptance.

If you have lost something or someone, she can help find those missing items, or guide us towards those people who are missing from our lives. She can help us find the purpose of our lives if we feel we have lost it.

She is associated with pure unconditional love relationships and world peace and is the guardian of the innocent.

Archangel Chamuel will guide psychologists and aestheticians and will support the employments of the police, prisons, hairdressers, social workers, the fashion industry, the fitness industry, surgeons, air traffic controllers, animal conservationists and peace keeping activists.

Chamuel is said to be a female Archangel, and is depicted as donning pink armour, and working through a ray of pink love and compassion to all those who ask for her help.

Associations:

- Virtue: Temperance
- Aura Colour: Ruby Red and Pale Green
- Scents: Mint, Geranium, Neroli and Ginger
- Day of the week: Tuesday
- Symbol: Heart
- Zodiac: Aries and Taurus
- Planet: Mars
- Element: Fire
- Chakra: Root
- Crystal: Red Jasper, Bloodstone, Carnelian, Pink Tourmaline, Rose Quartz

Archangel Jophiel

The name 'Jophiel' means 'beauty of God'.

Archangel Jophiel is the angel of beautiful thoughts, poetry, creative wisdom, understanding and judgement.

Jophiel is the patron of the arts and crafts, artistic and spiritual illumination and all creative pursuits. He provides clarity and understanding into the meaning and beauty of life, and creates insights as to our life purpose, encouraging positive thoughts and calm energy.

He is also the angel of homemaking and food, and thereby supports all kitchen gardens, vegetable patches, herb gardens and allotments, food preparation, food preservation and cooking.

He is tasked with the responsibility for the silent majority, in their campaigning and also assisting in the art of persuasion. He can shift perspective and use wisdom to help people see things from a different point of view and he will bring organisation to chaotic situations. He can change an outlook by helping us focus on the beauty that is already there, as yet unseen or unnoticed.

He can clear an overwhelmed mind to provide clarity of thought and can provide an awareness of abilities as yet unknown within us as individuals. He will assist those who are stuck in a rut of listlessness, boredom or depression, helping reignite our life's spark.

He is said to move at the speed of our thoughts, with a flight of high vibrational energy. His peaceful mind brings us serenity in our thoughts, enabling us to organise our work and home space to create a flow of calm energy and beauty to surrounding us.

His obligations are varied, including helping in matters of fashion, flowers and fragrances. He will always encourage us to present ourselves in our true authentic self, and not as someone else when choosing our appearance through make up, skin and hair care, enabling us to be rightly perceived by others for who we really are. He will help us see the beauty in life and in ourselves.

Other variations include his support of hikers, gardeners and musicians, being responsible for the great outdoors and the joy of music.

Among his many varied roles, he also assists in all forms of writing, journaling and blogging, encouraging truth and diversity, creativity and honesty in the written word. He supports artists and photographers through divine inspiration to guide artwork towards completion.

He is depicted as being very tall, wearing a yellow cloak and carrying the flaming sword of wisdom that frees us and enables free will. He will have a ray of golden yellow light surrounding him, often referred to as Jophiel's sunshine ray, which will bring forth joy, happiness and creative wisdom.

Associations:

- Virtue: Patience
- Aura Colour: Yellow
- Scents: Lavender, Orange, Myrrh and Lemon Grass

- Day of the week: Monday
- Zodiac: Libra
- Planet: Mercury and Venus
- Element: Air
- Chakra: Crown
- Crystal: Ametrine, Smokey Quartz and Rutilated Quartz

Archangel Uriel

The name 'Uriel' means 'light of God' or 'fire of God'. Archangel Uriel is also known as the Angel of Presence.

Archangel Uriel is the angel of salvation, illumination and wisdom and he resides among the illuminated seraphim.

He is the tasked with world peace, tranquillity, ceasefires and armistice. He is also concerned with fire, and fire protection, lightening, thunder and electricity.

He is the angel who guides the deceased towards the light of salvation.

He is associated with the physical movements and shifts of the Earth, such as earthquakes, volcanoes, floods and tsunamis. He looks after and heals the planet. He will assist with the continuous universal flow of the Earth's environment and is connected with the oceans, sea creatures, water levels, pollution, waste and salt.

Archangel Uriel controls the maps and knows the way.

He is depicted as a guide, holding a scroll in one hand upon which are all the answers to our life's path, and in the other hand he carries a staff or a bright lamp to help guide us along the true path of our lives.

He supports space exploration and is responsible for the mechanics of the universe, our solar system, eclipses, astronomy and astrology.

He assists with all forms of service and devotion, helping us learn to give as well as receive. He teaches us acceptance and he can show us how our lowest disappointments can become our greatest blessings. He can dispel feelings of anger, fear and despair, and move them into positive change and transformation towards a better state.

Archangel Uriel is also the patron of theatre, dance, music and literature. He will provide us with inspiration and intellect for the manifestation of new ideas.

He supports the thought processes we might need to find solutions to our questions, unblocking any obstacles within our thoughts and allowing us to draw our own conclusions through his guidance. He can purify our thoughts if we need help with understanding emotional and mental disturbances within our lives and provides a stabilising influence.

He will provide us with illumination within our thoughts, hearts and minds at the highest level, through his immense power and pure divine light, helping us find our own spiritual power, consciousness and enlightened spiritual understanding.

He is concerned with crafts, creative hobbies, magic and farming, by assisting with the notion of creating something new and discovering the depths of our true potential.

Archangel Uriel will always guide us towards promoting truth in any situation and he will assist in seeking out scams and schemes that are not honest.

He will aid writers, scribes, journalists and literacy as a whole in the promotion of honesty and truth through wisdom.

Associations:

- Virtue: Chastity
- Aura Colour: Red
- Scents: Sandalwood, Ginger and Basil
- Day of the week: Friday
- Direction: North
- Season: Summer

- Zodiac: Aquarius, Taurus, Virgo and Capricorn
- Planet: Uranus
- Element: Earth
- Chakra: Solar Plexus
- Crystal: Hematite, Obsidian, Tiger's Eye and Rutilated Quartz
- Tarot Card: The Tower Card

Archangel Zadkiel

The name 'Zadkiel' means 'righteousness of God'.

Archangel Zadkiel is the angel of joy, love, freedom and mercy and is also associated with comfort, prayer and abundance.

He is associated with change and transformation, where change is needed for good.

Archangel Zadkiel is considered to be the gentlest of all the Archangels. He is sometimes depicted as carrying the violet flame of righteousness, forgiveness and transmutation, or a dagger, surrounded by a blue or violet light.

He has the power to alter our negativity into a positive karma, bringing us tact and tolerance within the diversity of the ever changing world around us.

Archangel Zadkiel is also concerned with forgiveness, and assists us when we need to forgive ourselves or others to enable a personal relationship to move forward, even if the situation appears intolerable and impossible to forgive at first. He is the patron of those who forgive and will help us to come to terms with tragedy and others wrong doings towards us by releasing heavy emotions such as fear, anger and painful memories, and transmuting them back into love.

He supports all those involved with alternative, holistic and natural medicines, such as aromatherapists and reiki masters, guiding us towards choosing the most beneficial natural cure for our ails.

He will assist in improving our self-confidence when we feel it is ebbing away, bringing forth self-esteem and self-value, and developing our skills of persuasion and diplomacy to help navigate our way through any difficult or changing situations. He can guide us through the use of these skills towards spiritual and material abundance.

Archangel Zadkiel will also support human memory, when we need to remember a name, event or place from the past. He will assist with memory retention when faced with important exams and will assist with recollection during exam pressures. He is particularly associated with healing memory and cognitive functional disorders.

He is responsible for caring for all creatures that fly, including birds, insects, bats and butterflies.

Associations:

- Virtue: Kindness
- Aura Colour: Sky Blue and Violet
- Day of the week: Saturday

- Scents: Sandalwood, Ylang Ylang, Bergamot, Rosemary, and Nutmeg
- Zodiac: Gemini
- Planet: Jupiter
- Element: Air
- Chakra: Third Eye
- Crystal: Blue Lace Agate, Amethyst, Blue Chalcedony and Lapis Lazuli

Despite the title of this chapter, these Archangels are of no lesser importance than the seven principle Archangels. They are powerful angels of specific energies and guidance.

They are:

- Metatron
- Ariel
- Sandalphon
- Haniel
- Raziel
- Jeremiel
- Raguel
- Azrael

Archangel Metatron

Archangel Metatron is the angel of children and adolescents, both on Earth and in Heaven, and the angel of thought.

It is said, that Archangel Metatron was the human biblical prophet, Enoch, whom God ascended to the angelic realm for living a life of virtue and service to God.

As such, he represents the power and potential for man to ascend and to access spiritual enlightenment.

He is responsible for presiding over all guardian angels.

Archangel Metatron can support children through difficulties in school, and help resolve learning disorders and assist them as they grow towards adulthood.

He is also tasked with protecting and nurturing children with spiritual and psychic gifts, such as indigo, crystal and rainbow children.

He will assist with understanding through lateral thinking and supports people in construction industries such as architects, engineers and builders.

He will also support us when we choose a new path in life or take up a new opportunity, helping us grow and flourish in our new venture.

Archangel Metatron is appointed as God's scribe and he holds a direct link between our physical world and the angelic realm through Metatron's cube. He is often depicted as holding this cube in his hand and sometimes as holding a scroll and pen.

He is the head of the Akashic Records, or God's Archive and he is the holder and keeper of all knowledge of the universe.

Associations:

- Day: Sunday
- Element: Fire
- Planets: Pluto and the Sun
- Crystals: Sardonyx, Mahogany Obsidian and red or orange Aventurine.
- Zodiac: Virgo

Metatron's Cube

The Archangel Metatron created the cube out of his soul. It represents God's energy flowing through Metatron to all parts of creation. It is Metatron's task to ensure the energy flows in the proper balance so that nature will be in harmony. Through this cube, Metatron transmits the daily orders of God to Archangel Gabriel and Archangel Samuel.

Metatron's cube is an important symbol in sacred geometry. "Metatron's Cube generated the Platonic solids. These forms created structure throughout the universe." (Melchizedek, 2000).

Metatron's cube is depicted as a sacred geometric shape.

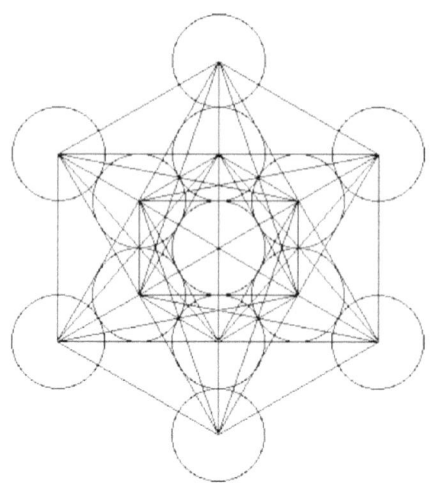

Metatron's Cube

The thirteen circles of this geometric shape represent the thirteen centres of energy in our human bodies, and the thirteen keys of creation.

The cube itself is a multi-dimensional map of the structure

of the universe, it's creation and formation, through the unlimited powerful flow of God's energy.

It is the gridwork of our consciousness and the building blocks of the cosmos. It is the matrix in which everything of our three dimensional reality is contained. (Tooley, 1997).

Archangel Ariel

The name 'Ariel' means 'Lion of God'.

Archangel Ariel is the patron of the environment and the animal kingdom, and those who care for it, such as environmentalists, vets, zookeepers and rangers.

He is tasked with protecting the ecosystems, animals, minerals and elemental forces, such as the winds and weathers of the Earth and will help in cleaning up after environmental disasters.

He is known to protect animals including pets and will assist us if we are trying to find a lost pet or in healing a sick or injured animal.

Archangel Ariel will assist us in reaping the rewards we are deserving of. When we form ideas, these are the seeds of future actions, events, creations and relationships. Ariel can help us grow these seeds into positive and productive fruition.

He can also guide us in our ability to provide good first impressions, which can then go on to form beneficial relationships with others in the future.

Using these skills, he can guide us towards material wealth and abundance by connecting us to a meaningful opportunity or coincidence, provided that our motivation is not one of greed.

He supports people who choose to travel and explore to connect with nature at a deeper level, providing insights and opportunities to expand our awareness and experience of the natural world.

He is also the guardian of nature spirits, such as faeries, sylphs and undines.

He is responsible for protecting the Earth's natural resources, such as water, food and shelter and to assist in the comfort and survival of mankind. He will help us find the materials things we need to live.

Associations:

- Planet: Saturn
- Element: Air
- Day: Saturday
- Crystals: Apatite, Agate and Jasper
- Zodiac: Aries

Archangel Sandalphon

Archangel Sandalphon is the patron angel of music, musicians, composers, poets and singers. He is also associated with strength, beauty and prosperity.

He is the deliverer of our prayers to God.

Similar to Enoch (Metatron), Archangel Sandalphon was the human biblical prophet Elijah who was ascended by God to the angelic realm.

The name 'Sandalphon' means 'brother', and he is considered the twin of Metatron.

He assists our understanding of the world and our life's path through music and tone, translating our thoughts through sound. Messages from Archangel Sandolphon will often be channelled through clairaudience. He can heal us through the use of music.

Archangel Sandalphon is also the guardian of the souls of unborn children. He is charged with watching over the processes of the natural world, and this includes the development of the unborn child in the womb. He helps with issues of fertility and conception. He also protects the mother and child throughout pregnancy and will assist in the safety of the mother and child during delivery. He supports midwives, nurses and paediatricians.

In line with his musical connection, he can provide creative inspiration to musicians by clearing away mental and emotional blocks. He can remove fear, guilt and aggressive tendencies that can impede a creative flow.

He is associated with the colours of nature, and is responsible for the changing seasons, such as the changing colours of the leaves in autumn and the deep blue of a summer sky. Through these natural colours, Archangel Sandalphon can heal the illnesses and ailments of mankind and sustain and protect us from further ails, promoting health and wellbeing.

He is tasked with being the protector of the earth and is responsible for the health and welfare of mankind.

Associations:

- Planet: Jupiter
- Element: Earth
- Day: Thursday
- Crystal: Turquoise and Calcite.
- Zodiac: Pisces

Archangel Haniel

The name "Haniel' means 'Glory of God', 'Joy of God', or 'Grace of God' and he is the angel of divine communication, growth, love and healing.

Archangel Haniel is responsible for water, and also for awareness of mood. He helps us develop through our emotions, intuitions and imagination.

He is the angel of life force energy, vibrant well-being and passion for life.

When we feel an atmosphere or a situation that we are unable to fully comprehend, Archangel Haniel can provide insight towards reality. He can cleanse away worry and guide us back to truth.

Archangel Haniel has a gentle nurturing energy that can soothe and heal when we are in a challenging situation or experiencing heavy emotions such as anxiety and worry.

He can also help women during monthly cycles and with symptoms of menopause.

He can assist us to reach our true potential height, by creating positive change and bestowing luck, harmony, protection and grace.

He is often depicted as wearing a turquoise robe and holding a pearly blue and white orb of healing light which can enhance our intuition and psychic abilities. He has two impressive large silver wings.

He can been seen in our visions, dreams and meditations as a beneficial turquoise light providing a feeling of joy, strength and spiritual guidance during times of weakness.

He can provide us with clear articulation and inspiration when we need to be able to effectively communicate, such as during an interview or presentation.

Associations:

- Planet: Moon and Venus
- Chakra: Throat
- Day: Friday
- Element: Water
- Crystals: Rose Quartz, Pink Calcite and Chrysoprase.

Archangel Raziel

The name 'Raziel' means 'Secrets of God'.

Archangel Raziel hears all the secret knowledge of God about the universe and heaven. He is the

Keeper of God's secrets and the angel of the mysteries of life. He is said to have collated all of God's secrets in a book called the Sefer Raziel, which he revealed to Adam, the first man, and also to Noah during the Great Flood.

He is the angel who will restore the spark and zest for life when it has been lost. He supports us when we live life to the full, in honesty and truth.

Archangel Raziel is the patron of law and lawyers, astrologers, scientists, clairvoyants and secret service workers.

He can heal ails such as headaches, migraines, eyesight problems and sinus pains. He can also help with pituitary, thyroid and other glandular problems, and reduce and remove tumours and growths, and assist with diagnosing the root of an illness.

His calming influence can soothe backpains, kidney disease and reduce blood pressure.

As the guardian of mystical knowledge, he brings the intention of magic, magical teachings and healing and will assist in our dream interpretations and psychic learning.

Archangel Raziel will assist us when we are faced with a mystery, puzzle or conundrum, guiding us towards a solution whether they be abstract, emotional, spiritual or physical. He is connected with all the mysteries of the universe.

He can often appear as a shadow, but then may also communicate through divine lights in the sky and meditations and visions, Archangel

Raziel can guide us towards enhanced understanding of all things spiritual and also with psychic development.

Associations:

- Chakra: Throat and Crown
- Crystal: Peridot, Apache Tears and Aqua Aura Crystals
- Planet: Neptune
- Day: Saturday
- Element: Air
- Zodiac: Leo

Archangel Jeremiel

The name 'Jeremiel' means 'mercy of God'.

Archangel Jeremiel assists us with transformations in life. He is the angel of emotions. He guides us through important and difficult life changes, such as births, deaths and marriages, divorces and separations.

When we are struggling with the death of someone close, he will provide space for contemplation and mourning. When we are overwhelmed by the joy of a new birth or wedding, he will provide space for celebration.

Archangel Jeremiel is tasked with assisting the souls of the dead in reviewing their lives.

He will tend to communicate through dreams, visions and symbols and is often known as the angel of dreams.

He can help us let go of the past and embrace valuable life lessons, bringing a sense of clarity of thought to clear negative emotions. He allows us to take stock of our thoughts, guiding us towards unblocking our intuitions and spiritual awareness which may have been impeded by past traumas or unpleasant experiences, and moving us towards a more positive enlightened state of mind.

He will assist us in reviewing our living lives and encouraging a loving respectful nature towards ourselves and all others.

He will deliver mercy when it is asked for.

Associations:

- Crystal: Amethyst
- Planet: Pluto
- Zodiac: Scorpio

Archangel Raguel

The name 'Raguel' means 'friend of God'.

Archangel Raguel is the angel of order, fairness and harmony. He will help weigh the balance in any given situation and find a fair solution.

His is also the angel of snow and ice and he is depicted as carrying a flaming sword with which he can melt the snow of winter.

He will intervene when you feel you have been dealt with unjustly. He will assist in unravelling confused feelings and will guide us towards the correct path to take when we feel lost.

He will also assist us in making new friends and healing rifts between old friends. He creates harmony and understanding in relationships.

Associations:

- Crystal: Milky Quartz and Moonstone
- Zodiac: Sagittarius

Archangel Azrael

The name 'Azrael' means 'whom God helps'.

Archangel Azrael is the patron of religious leaders, clerics, priests and masters.

He assists with all human choices over transitions and changes, such as gender changes. He intervenes by offering both sides of every story, showing the outcome of each possible choice of path, and then allowing us to use freewill to make an informed choice of which path to follow.

When we reach a major crossroads in our lives, such as in career or relationships, and we have to make an important decision, Archangel Azrael is there to help us make the right choice to enable us to lead the best possible life.

Archangel Azrael has also been called the Angel of death, as he is tasked with the role of offering comfort, compassion and love at the moment of death. He acts as a bridge between the human world and the spirit world, assisting humans in transition from death to the afterlife.

He is known to be quiet, strong, patient and compassionate and will use these qualities to be there to offer guidance and healing to those who are left behind to grieve emotionally, surrounding them in a warm comforting white light.

He supports helpers, carers, healers and counsellors.

Associations:

- Day: Tuesday
- Planet: Mars
- Element: Earth
- Zodiac: Capricorn
- Crystals: Yellow Calcite, Amethyst and Purple Fluorite

Guardian Angels

Guardian angels come from the third order of angels in the third sphere of the angel hierarchy.

A guardian angel is assigned to every individual living soul on the Earth, from the moment of conception until death when they will guide the soul towards the eternal light on their passage to the afterlife.

They are an ever present link between ourselves and God. Like all angels, they exist in their own space, residing in the angelic realm, yet they still remain with us at all times. They are created by God and their mission is to guide and protect us through deliverance of God's ministration.

Your Guardian Angel

Your guardian angel's primary function is to protect you from spiritual and physical evil. They will help and guide you, and you alone. No one else. They are for you exclusively. You are their sole priority. They are faithful, prudent and powerful, and their love for God and God's love for you directs them to always love and watch over you.

There are many references to guardian angels in the Bible. Here are three:

Matthew 18:10

Beware that you don't look down on any of these little ones. For I tell you that in heaven, their angels are always in the presence of my Heavenly Father.

Psalm 90:11

For he (God) hath given his angels charge over thee, to keep thee in all thy ways.

Psalm 91:10-12

No disaster can overtake you, no plague come near your tent; he (God) has given his angels orders about you to guard you wherever you go. They will carry you in their arms in case you trip over a stone.

Although you have your own unique guardian angel, you are of course free to ask for assistance from other angels also. Your guardian angel will still be there with you, and will work with the angel you have called upon to help resolve whatever issue you requested them for.

Your guardian angel will always love you, no matter what you do in your life. They will always stand by you and be there to offer help whenever you ask. They know you completely. The have been with you for your entire life and they fully understand you.

Your guardian angel can act upon your senses and your imagination, encouraging you to make the right decisions, but they will not interfere with your fate or your freewill. They will help and protect you, but if you choose not to listen to them and take another path, they will not stop you.

As with all angels within the angel hierarchy, your guardian angel will not help you do any harm to yourself or others. Neither will they assist you in doing things that are wrong or bad. All angels are created by God and they must keep his law. For example, they will not assist you in robbing a bank. Neither will they help you commit suicide. But they will still always be there for you.

Getting To Know Your Guardian Angel

Most people are completely unaware of the presence their guardian angel. Many will even deny their existence. A guardian angel will not openly reveal themselves. If you choose to deny them, it will be as if they are staying quiet. They may still try to assist through angelic communication, such as coincidences, synchronicities and signs, but denying their existence will probably leave you unaware and oblivious to their aid.

They are there to help do as you ask, and so it is you who decides whether your guardian angel will reveal themselves. If you choose, you can develop a profound relationship with your guardian angel. They are ready for you and waiting for you to ask.

Ask Your Guardian Angel To Reveal Himself To You

You can openly ask your guardian angel to reveal himself.

Incidentally, as with all angels, your guardian angel maybe male or female. You will come to know this. Angels do not technically have a specific gender, but through our knowledge and experience, we come to attach gender to them. This gender is a human perspective of the angels.

Making a conscious choice to connect with your guardian angel is the first step. It must be a clear definite decision. An adamant belief in the knowledge of his existence and an acceptance that he is always there for you.

Sit alone, in a comfortable position, in a quiet room. The temperature should be ambient. The atmosphere must be calm.

Close your eyes.

Slow your breathing. Draw in each breath slowly and deeply and let each breath out just as slowly. Listen only to the sound of your breathing.

When you are ready, there is no rush, just take your time, say out loud, "I ask that my guardian angel comes to me. I ask that he reveals himself. And I thank my guardian angel for his presence."

Continue to breathe slowly. Focus on your every breath.

Now start to focus on other things. Listen to other sounds. Maybe a distant hum of a road, or birds singing, or something else.

As you draw in your breath, notice what you can smell. A gentle scent maybe? What can you taste?

Continue to breathe slowly and consider how you feel. Are you warm? What sensations do you feel? Do you have any emotional responses? Are you calm? Are you happy? Are you sad?

What can you see in your mind? What colours do you see? Are the colours changing? What else can you see? Are people, places or objects forming?

Slowly open your eyes, but remain unfocused and calm for a few moments. Allow the calm channels of energy flow to remain open. You have opened yourself up to connect with your guardian angel and they are with you and ready to assist you in whatever you ask.

If you are requesting assistance for something specific, now is the time to ask. Be open and honest about what help you need. Say it out loud. And then be thankful for the assistance you will be given. Express your gratitude out loud. Your guardian angel will hear you and will help and guide you.

Now re-focus your eyes and return your breathing to normal.

You may have experienced a spiritual moment during this exercise. This moment will be individual and unique to you. Only you can describe it and it will be different for every person. This will be your guardian angel connecting with you. You may even be beginning to feel their presence.

If you did not have any spiritual sensation, don't worry, they were still there and you will know at some point over the next few days. You will feel them.

Your guardian angel will also choose to show themselves through other means, such as coincidences, synchronicities and signs, which I will go on to explain later. They may use these methods to offer you comfort, guidance or protection and to answer your request for help.

Some people choose to name their guardian angel. You may choose a male or female name, however you know your guardian angel to be. You will feel their gender. You will be able to visualise them in your mind's eye. You will find the name that is right. It is your choice and it will come to you.

Naming your guardian angel gives us a sense of differentiating them from other angels that we may connect with. It helps develop our personal relationship with them.

You must tell your guardian angel their name, so that you can call on their name when you next request their help.

People of religious faith may know the following 12th century prayer which can be made to your guardian angel, acknowledging, appreciating and requesting his assistance through life:

12th Century Guardian Angel Prayer

Angel of God

My Guardian dear

To whom his love

Commits me here

Ever this day

Be at my side

To light and guard

To rule and guide

Amen

As previously stated in the chapter on the seven principle Archangels, there was a great war in heaven, started by an angel called Lucifer.

A multitude of angels, so many in fact that their number is unimaginable to humans, were created by God and given by him their free will. One of the most beautiful and intelligent of these angels was Lucifer. The name Lucifer means 'light bearer', and he was referred to as the 'morning star'.

Lucifer was aware of his extreme beauty and intelligence and fell foul to the sin of pride and disobedience to his creator. Forgetting that he was a creature made by God, designed to serve

God and act as a messenger to God's people, he rebelled at the idea of being subjected to serve. So with a greed for power, he led a revolt, followed by about a third of the heavenly angels, to replace God, and war broke out in Heaven.

Defeated by the Archangels and God's omniscient power and authority, God expelled Lucifer and his angels who had followed him from heaven. They were cast down to Earth and became known as the fallen angels.

Revelations, 12:8

There was no longer any place for them in heaven.

Isaiah, 14:12

How you have fallen from heaven.
O morning star, son of the dawn!
You have been cast down to earth.

As leader of the fallen angels, Lucifer goes by many names, including Satan, the Devil, Beelzebub, the dragon, the serpent, and the father of lies. His followers, the fallen angels, are also referred to as demons, evil, and unclean spirits.

God has created all beings, both angelic and human, with free will and two choices; either to accept his authority over evil, or to follow Satan into evil.

Satan and his fallen angels will try to corrupt and destroy all that is good and godly, to separate humans from God, drawing them away from truth and light, as he knows God loves us.

While God has all power and control, he has promised us free will. Satan and evil will test us with temptation, accusation and deception. They will look for and exploit weakness within humans, destructive weaknesses such as pride, greed and lust.

But we have a strength. We simply have to remember that we have God's angels to help us, guide us and protect us. They are always willing and waiting to help. We have free will and we have a choice. All we have to do is ask for guidance.

God created all beings and then gave them free will. This means that when faced with any kind of decision, you are free to choose your own path.

The angels also have free will. They have made their choice.

The fallen angels have chosen to follow Satan and they will tempt you, in many different ways, and many times, towards the wrong path drawing you away from your true destiny, testing the depth of your faith in what is right and good.

The heavenly angels have chosen to reside with God, as loving benevolent messengers of God, protecting and guiding us towards all that is good in truth and light, to lead full, rewarding, wholesome and worthwhile lives. This is the path to happiness, completion and contentedness.

For us to be able to make a choice, we must have faith. We must have a belief in what is right and good, and a knowledge or awareness of there being consequences to all our actions.

Faith is our human way of believing in something we cannot and may never be able to prove.

As humans, we have to accept that fully understanding the concept of angels is beyond our earthly capability. When we consider them and imagine them, we apply our human concepts, because that is the only reference we have to draw on. We picture them in human shape and form. We attach to them human attributes and abilities. We do this because we simply do not have the slightest level comprehension to properly describe or imagine the angelic existence. Therefore, we have to accept our inability to understand and have faith.

When angels reveal themselves to us, they can choose to appear in human form. But this is not their true form. Their true form is beyond our capable vision. Neither are they with us as we see them. They reside in their own space and with no constraints of time. They can be in all places and all times. Always ready and willing to help. Having faith is the only way we can grasp this.

Faith can be underpinned and strengthened by being open to recounts of how angels have helped people. There are numerous examples to be found, from all over the world, of the intervention of angels for the betterment of humans, protecting them from danger, healing them from illness, and helping them achieve and succeed.

When you have faith, you can then use your gift of free will to make the right choices.

With your faith in place, when you ask for help in any situation, the angels will communicate a response with guidance and encouragement towards the right path to take. But it will still be your choice whether to take it or not. That is your free will.

Coincidences, Synchronicities and Signs

Do we have full understanding or control over every single event in our lives?

Sometimes things happen for which we have no rational explanation. They could be random. But sometimes it can be surprisingly well timed. And there are times when something very simple will occur, that you will notice, to which there is no earthly human logical reasoning. This is when an angel is communicating with you, through coincidences, synchronicities and signs.

Coincidences

Coincidences occur when two events, which have nothing presently to do which each other, happen within a very short space of time, and then a link between them becomes apparent retrospectively.

When you ask for help from an angel, or even acknowledge your faith in angels, coincidences start to happen. The more you look for them, the more you recognise them happening.

Coincidence is God's way of remaining anonymous

- *Albert Einstein*

There are three types of coincidences.

Sign Coincidences

Some coincidences are signs that occur soon after a request for help from an angel has been made.

For example, you may have asked for help to heal a sick child, and then very soon after, you see a feather float down in front of you, from no apparent source, or a light brush against your arm, when there is no-one there. This is a coincidence. It is a communication from an angel to show they have heard your request and they are sharing with you their intention to help you.

Right Time Coincidences

Other coincidences are called right time coincidences. These are where several related situations happen within a short space of time.

For example, you may have asked an angel for guidance on coping with a broken relationship. Very soon a song plays on the radio that capsulises how you are feeling. Or the phone rings and it is an old friend ringing for a chat. Or someone new unexpectedly enters your life in a random way. These are communications and interventions from your angel, providing guidance and help.

Right Place Coincidences

Another form of coincidences are right place coincidences. These occur when you just happen to be in the right place for a situation that you have asked for to be played out.

For example, you may have asked an angel for help to find a job as a receptionist. Very soon, you go to a friend's BBQ and happen to meet with a friend whose brother is looking for a receptionist for his company. Or, you are having your hair cut at your regular hairdressers and the receptionist there tells you she is leaving and they need to fill her position. Or you might be having a coffee in a café, and there is a newspaper left on your table. The first page you turn to has an advert for your perfect job. This is angelic intervention, clearing the way and helping you to follow the path you have chosen. Your angel has ensured everything is in place to guide you.

Synchronicities

Synchronicity involves synchronous timing. It is when two separate events occur at the same time, which have meanings emerge when viewed together.

The sum of the whole is greater than the sum of the parts

-The Theory of Synergy

When one thing happens, it can be considered as chance. But when two or more things happen at the same time, that is angelic intervention and communication.

For example, you may have asked an angel to reassure that you are following the right path for your life. Very soon, your favourite song plays on the radio. At the same time, a rainbow appears in the sky, it stops raining, the sun comes out and a small child randomly waves at you. These events are synchronised by your angel to provide you with the reassurance you requested. You will know. You will find yourself smiling inside and overcome by a feeling of calm.

Signs

Signs can occur within coincidences or synchronous events, but they can also occur on their own. They can be one off events, created by angels to help, guide or protect you.

These signs may be direct and obvious or indirect and more subtle. But the more you look for them, the more you will get used to recognising them and the more often you will see them.

It might be something you see, feel or tangibly touch, and when you find yourself saying, "It's a sign", then your intuition is right. This is you accepting communication from an angel.

Some signs will be personal, and will only have meaning for you. But you will see and understand them if you look. They tell us the angels are near and they give us a message to interpret.

Some common signs are often used by angels to communicate their presence.

Feathers

If you see a feather in an unusual place, or it floats down to you unexpectedly, then an angel is letting you know of their presence. It may be any size, shape or colour, and it may be in response to your request for assistance, or simply to reassure or comfort you during a difficult time. A white feather will arrive at a time when you are most in need, to let you know you are not alone.

Rainbows

Rainbows have well known scientific explanations. But have you ever stared at a rainbow and still felt the magic? Maybe it's shape does not look quite right, or it has occurred without rain, or it has happened at a time soon after you have asked for a sign to reassure or reaffirm some situation in your life. It may be a double rainbow or a rainbow orb or halo around an object. The angels are using this phenomenon to guide you.

Bells

If you can hear a bell ring, even the slightest tinkle or chirp of a bell, and there is no apparent reason for a bell to ring, then an angel is near you.

Voices

You may think you have heard someone lightly call your name when there is no one around. Or you may hear a word, or several words. It may be that you hear a voice, but cannot understand the words that are being spoken. Ask the angel to speak clearer or louder, so you can hear and understand them. It is usually a quiet voice, often a whisper, a calm serene tone of assurance, that is letting you know of the caring presence of an angel.

Coins

A single coin in an unusual place signifies an angel is near. If it is on the pavement of a road you were thinking of walking down, then do so. If it is on the doorstep of a building, shop or home, then enter it. These are signs being left for you by an angel who wishes to guide you along your path.

Also, you may find when you look carefully at a coin that you have found or that someone has given you, that it may have an image or numbers that resonate with some profound meaning for you.

Changes in the Localised Climate

When angels are very present, the localised climate around you may alter. The temperature may get slightly warmer or cooler, but still remaining comfortable. The light may appear just a little brighter, or the room and its furnishings may ever so slightly glow, almost unnoticeably so. The air might feel only the slightest bit heavier and you might notice not much more than a tingle of a movement of the air around you. If you were not open to the idea of angels, if you

189

did not have faith, you would not even notice these changes, but by being spiritually aware, you will come to notice when the presence of angels affect the local environment surrounding you.

Media

If you have requested assistance from an angel, there is every possibility they could provide guidance by directing you to an answer to be found within media. You may come across a relevant thread in social media, or a helpful answer on the TV, without having been intentionally looking there for answers. It may be that you notice a message on a local bill board or a certain street name or shop sign. It will hold a meaning for you. The angels can use any avenue of communication to connect with you.

Clouds

Seeing specific shapes in clouds, such as hearts and other shapes, can be signs of guidance. You may even be able to see the shape of an angel or angel wings, a sure sign that they are there for you.

Lights and Orbs

Angels exude pure divine light. Orbs are said to be 'vehicles of angels'. These are opaque spherical features which usually present themselves in photos, but which can also be observed by the naked eye. Sometimes you may see a shower of light, a shimmer, sparkle, flash or an orb, of any colour, in the corner of your eye, but when you look directly at it, it's not there. You should believe in what you have noticed. It has caught your eye for a reason. It may be an unusual shimmer of light off an object, like an unfocused reflection of something that isn't there. This is the presence of an angel.

Feelings

Angels may communicate with us through our sixth sense, our psychic abilities. You may become aware of the presence of angels through clairvoyance, clairaudience, or any of the other spiritual abilities. Remember, you can work on improving these abilities and increase you spiritual awareness of angels.

You may simply 'feel' the presence of an angel. You may experience a subtle brush across your arm or neck. Or the placement of a hand on your back or shoulder. You may sense the presence of someone with you when you are in an empty room. You may feel emotionally and inexplicably loved. This is when an angel has wrapped you in the comfort of their wings, surrounding you with the protection and comfort of their purest love. Trust this feeling. It is real. It doesn't lie to you. It is truth.

Wing Symbols

Images of angelic wings are signs of angels, such as wings drawn in dust or sand, or in the condensation on a window pane.

Music

Rarely, you may find yourself hearing angelic music or singing from no apparent source. This is angelic communication.

Also, angels might use music to guide you or comfort you. You might find yourself listening to a piece of music that can change your mood, or provide a specific meaning to you. Or you may notice a recurring piece of music playing, or several pieces of music with similar themes. It could be that a particular piece of music invokes an old memory of a place or a person and this maybe a sign that you should re-visit this place or contact that person. Sometimes a song may just start playing in your mind. Embrace this. This is angelic intervention on your behalf, for your benefit.

Clock Chimes

Sometimes you may notice a clock chime, or part chime, or even just give a slight ping, when it is not supposed to. When this happens, an angel is near you.

Scent

You may suddenly smell a fragrance or scent, that has no apparent origin. This is a sign of an angel near you. It may be flowery, it will always be pleasant, and it might invoke a memory. If it does, then the angel near you has deliberately wanted you to remember something for a reason. You may even find you have a recurrent unexplained fragrance that you may come to recognise as that of a specific angel, maybe your guardian angel.

Babies, Young Children and Pets

You may notice that sometimes babies and young children will suddenly look in a particular direction and laugh or clap or even seem to be communicating with something that to us, as adults, is not there. Similarly, your pet might notice something, or bark at something when there is seemingly nothing there. They are responding to the presence of angels. Their pure untainted innocence and unquestioning love allows them to

be able to connect at a higher
spiritual level.

Objects Falling

Sometimes, an object may fall out
in front of you. It may be a book
falling off a shelf. Or a ring falls
from the table. Maybe a coin drops
from your purse. In every case,
carefully regard the item. What is
the title of the book? Did it fall
open on a particular page? What is
the significance of the ring? What
does it bring to mind? What does
the image, wording or numbers on
the coin mean to you? Whatever it
is that has fallen before you, it will
hold a meaning that you will be
able to identify with. It is the
guiding intervention of an angel,
leading you to an answer or

solution to something on your mind.

Dreams

When an angel visits you in a dream, listen to them. They may be giving you a message. Or maybe they want to lead you somewhere in your dream. Go with them. They are with you and they are trying to offer you some kind of guidance, maybe to answer a question you have asked or to help you find the correct path to take, or to protect you.

Repetition

Angels can use repetition of an event to draw your attention. For example, if you hear the same name repeated by three unrelated people within a matter of days, then this may be a sign from the angels that you should get in touch with that person. Hence the phrase, *pay attention when things happen in threes.* (White, L, nd).

As your faith grows and your spiritual awareness strengthens, you will learn to look for signs and be open to receiving them. Connection and communication with angels will become easier and more commonplace. They will find ways to guide you, protect you, and assist you in your requests for help, always leading you on your correct path, helping you find the true value and meaning of your life.

Yet you still have freewill. You are not forced to follow the guidance of angels. They cannot control you and they cannot stop you from taking an opposing path to the one they suggest. It is your choice. But know, that the angels will always be working for you, never against you and they will always do their best for you.

Always pay attention. Always be open and ready to recognise and acknowledge a sign and the presence of an angel. And always express your gratitude for their time, interest and divine love for you.

How many times have you glanced at the clock and noticed an unusual number such as 11.11? Have you ever woken unexpectedly, with no idea what woke you, checked the clock and again, it's an unusual number, such as 5:55? Or a number that just pricks your consciousness but you don't know why? It may not be a clock. It may be a number plate on a car that says 123, or a page number that a book has randomly fallen open on, say page 333, or a supermarket bill of £22.22, or any number that you just happen to notice anywhere.

When these numbers are in a sequence of three or more, they are examples of angelic communication. The angels are connecting with you. Some are specific numbers which I will go on to explain. But sometimes it will be any number that is only relevant to you. If it resonates with your mind or thoughts, then it is an angel communicating. You will know and understand it if you take the time to notice and think about it. Sometimes it's relevance will not become obvious at first, but in time, it will.

Numerology is the study of the meaning of numbers and their relationship with coincidental events. According to worldnumerology.com, 'the art of numerology is based on the personality of numbers'. The usage of numerology as a spiritual science can be traced back to the early Egyptians and Babylonians.

Angel numbers have specific meanings applied to them.

Angel Number Meanings

0 = Guidance is available for you from the angels and they are waiting for you to ask. They are ready to assist you in your journey of spiritual awakening.

1 = This is the number of unity, permanence and foundation. It represents originality, independence and leadership. Something new and original may be about to begin in your life. Look on the bright side, be positive and the result will be a yes answer.

2 = This is the number of natural duality and it represents cooperation, association and sensitivity towards others. Another person will bring the result to you. You must look out for them.

3 = This is the number of harmony and balance. It represents spirituality, creativity and self-expression. Your life is harmonious now and your path ahead is clear to see if you look. Avenues of creativity are opening up for you.

4 = This is the number of the root of all things. It represents stability, work and career. Your challenges are of your own making. You need to take a step back from a situation to be able to fully understand it.

5 = This is the number is equilibrium and manifestation. It represents adventure, excitement and higher consciousness. Your own genius wants to be heard. Listen carefully to all your own thoughts as therein lies the path to growth and truth.

6 = This is the number of perfection. It represents home, family and responsibility. Smaller components, hints and clues will bring a whole situation together. Look more deeply for them.

7 = This is the number of unification. It represents your alignment with your true life's path and spiritual purpose. You are lucky and you can now expand your empire. Avenues of opportunity will open up to you and much can be achieved when you cooperate with another.

8 = This is the number of birth and re-birth. It represents abundance and material prosperity. Build solid foundations. Keep your secrets and those of others. Be discrete.

9 = This number of boundary and limitation. It represents your

deeper spiritual purpose. Raise your horizons to see the bigger picture. Increase your beliefs, dreams and visions of your future and further your boundaries.

Master Angel Number Meanings

11 = You are an individual in the purest form. You should listen to your deepest spiritual purpose.

13 = You are ascending through powerful new beginnings.

22 = You can gain through joining with others. You will then have what you need to make your dreams come true.

33 = You already know the answer. You must truly believe in your spiritual self to find it.

1111 = You have an opportunity to expand, grow and achieve. Embrace this opportunity.

1212 = You must stay focused and optimistic of your brightest possible future and so it will happen.

1122 = You have the energy and skill to achieve your life's purpose. Self-belief is your strength.

Identical Numbers

A sequence of three or more identical numbers shown to you unexpectedly is a way for angels to get you to stop and pay attention. They are trying to tell you something. You need to ponder what is on your mind at that time, or what the number refers to. Take the meaning of the first number and consider it to be strengthened by its repetition. It has been highlighted by the angels, to underline it's significance and make it more urgent or important in your life. Pay attention to it. The answer is within you. The angels are using the identical sequence to guide you.

Unique Numbers

As an individual, you will also have a unique number that angels will use to connect with you, to make you aware of something. You may not know your unique number, but the angels will have presented it to you in the past, and they will do again. It is for you to notice and become aware of. It will be a random three digit number that keeps popping up unexpectedly in your life.

There will be other numbers, of not necessarily just three digits, that will only hold a relevance to you personally when you see them because you can refer them to something specific in your life. For example, maybe you keep seeing the numbers of the house where you grew up, or the numbers within your date of birth. Again, the angels are letting you know of their presence. They are offering you guidance and support.

Number Manipulation

Another typical angelic communication can come from patterns of numbers, or a relevance emerging from a manipulation of numbers, such as the 216th number of the Fibonacci sequence described later.

An example of manipulation is when all numbers in a sequence are eventually added to result in one number. For example, the number 854 has the same meaning as the number 8, because 8 + 5 + 4 = 17 and then 1 + 7 = 8.

Number Patterns

To one person, a pattern of numbers may mean nothing, but to another person, a certain pattern may make them take note and pay attention. They may not know why, but with time and thought, the meaning will become apparent. For example, it may be a run of numbers that are all even or all odd. Or it may be a pattern such as

1,3,5,7... or any pattern that you recognise.

In fact, anything that appears to be a pattern to you, that makes you sit up and take note, is an angelic intervention, an invite from an angel letting you know that they are there, ready to help, guide and support you. It may not necessarily even be numeric, it may be any form of pattern, presenting itself from any corner of your material life, be they alphabetic, colour, sound, visual etc etc. Be spiritually aware. Take time to listen and notice. Before long, you will be seeing many patterns around you and you will be feeling the strong presence of loving angels supporting and guiding along the true path of your life. And it will be an immensely powerful and uplifting awakening experience.

Scarcity and Quantity

When an amount is very small, it feels important and desirable. Similarly, when an amount is vast, it feels extraordinary and impressive. This is scarcity and quantity. In both cases, the scarcity and quantity creates the value.

Scarcity of Angels

Some angels are known individually. We know of our guardian angel. We know of specific angels such as the Archangels, a select group of individual angels identifiable by name, each with special certain skills and associations.

These are examples of scarcity. They are small groups to which we attach high importance.

Quantity of Angels

In contrast, the total number of angels is a vast humanly unimaginable number.

Aside from the Archangels, in other choirs, the number of angels is immense, too many for our limited human minds to even begin to contemplate. This is referred to as multitudes of angels.

In the lowest choir of regular angels there are legions upon legions upon legions of angels. A legion is said to be up to 6000 angels, based on the Roman definition of a legion. Therefore, there are 6000 x 6000 x 6000 angels, in this choir, which totals 216,000,000,000 angels.

Incidentally, and slightly deviating from the topic, in sacred geometry, there is a geometric number sequence called the Fibonacci Numbers, first recognised by Pingala, circa 250 BC. The 216th number in the Fibonacci sequence is 6192204516665901352286753878 6329787426939612 and if you add up all these individual numbers, they add up to 216. An interesting coincidence in itself. But there's more: This specific number is significant in many cultures, and it is believed the hidden name of God contains 216 characters (Brewer, 2019). And this is an example of another numerical coincidence; an angelic connection to the total number of regular angels in the last choir as described in the previous paragraph.

So far we have learnt about the different angels ready to help us, their associations, and how they would show us they are there. But how do we actually invoke their attention and ask for help and/or protection?

First of all, it is important to know, that anyone and everyone can call upon the angels. Beliefs, gender, race, age, or any other human attribute is irrelevant to angels. They will assist mankind as individuals and as a whole. They can help with any aspect of your daily life, be it of major importance or something that is less significant. For example, you might ask for

- Help to elevate your spiritual awareness
- Healing of a jealousy, grief or other emotional pain
- Help retrieving a lost object
- Help finding love
- Comfort in loneliness
- Help getting a job
- Physical healing after an accident
- Protection for your family, friends, loved ones and yourself
- Strength to be forgiving
- Understanding of your spiritual path and life purpose
- Help finding joy in life.

Etc etc.

Clearing Toxic Energy

Before invoking the help of an angel, you should start to clear away any toxic energy within you. Spiritually, this could be thoughts, people, relationships or situations of the past that have left you with emotional and spiritual baggage.

Over the course of your life so far, you will have been taught ways to live, by your parents, carers, peers, religious teachers, media and any other avenues that have affected you. You will have been taught their beliefs and these will be with you, whether consciously or unconsciously. They will have given you prejudices and discriminations and until now, these have sustained and maintained you.

You will, to a point, already have consciously evaluated and chosen which beliefs you align with and which you discard. But to invoke the angels, you must delve deeper to find yourself, your own true ideals, untainted by the baggage of the past.

You may not be able to straight away pin point which taught beliefs are not right for you, they will become apparent over time. But as each one presents itself, and you come to recognise it as toxic, then you must cleanse it away. You must admit that it no longer serves you and give yourself absolute permission to discard it from your life. Visualise the belief as a heavy black ball and throw it into the sea. Visualise it sinking deep deep away until it no longer has any standing within your thoughts.

Eventually you will learn and understand your own set of beliefs. Stay true to them and do not let others distract you from them. Live your spiritual life consciously, and in the present. You are a unique human individual and the loving angels will support, protect, assist and guide you.

Which Angels to Connect With

There are two types of angels that we may call upon. The Archangels by name, and the regular angels from the third choir of the third sphere. Remember, there are legions upon legions upon legions of them ready to help, and you may have many angels helping you at any one time.

If you call upon the regular angels to assist you with a task, once the task is complete, they will leave. But your guardian angel will always stay with you.

We would not normally call upon angels from the other choirs.

You would ask for the assistance of an Archangel if you feel that the Archangel is particularly associated with the task at hand and hence will be more directly able to help.

You can refer back to the Archangels described earlier in this book to see which are most suited for the task you need help with.

Connect with angels

To connect with angels is simple. They have always been there for you and are waiting for you.

Sit alone, in a quiet room.

The temperature should be ambient and you should be calm and comfortable.

Close your eyes.

Relax your mind and slow your breathing.

Breathe deeply in and out, slowly.

Listen to the sound of your breathing.

This is your relaxed state.

Say out loud, "I ask that the angels connect with me. I ask that the angels are near me. I ask that the angels stay with me. I thank the angels for hearing me."

They angels have heard you and are there.

When you are ready, open your eyes. Take your time.

You have connected with angels. They are with you and ready to assist you with anything you need.

This is the start of your spiritual awareness of angels.

If you do not wish to speak out loud when you connect, you can focus your thoughts and say the words in your head, as in a prayer.

Active, Passive, Resist

When you ask an angel for assistance, their response may be active, passive or resistive. The response you receive will be the right response for you.

Active:

When you ask an angel to help bring something specific into your life, or to manifest something, they may choose to respond actively. For example, if you have asked for help to find someone to love, they may actively and obviously direct you through various signs, coincidences and synchronicities.

Passive

It may be, that a suitable response to your request for help may be that of watching. For example, if you have asked that they watch over you for protection, they will react actively should it become necessary, but for now, a passive response it correct. Similarly, you may have asked for help to follow your true spiritual path. The angels will remain passive, lingering near you, until it becomes necessary to become active to maintain your request through signs, coincidences and synchronicities.

Resist

When you ask for help with something that is not good for you, that may cause you or someone else harm, or that may be considered wrong, the angels may choose to put obstacles in your way.

For example, say you have applied for a job. You have asked the angels to help you get this specific job. But the time of the interview is set at the same time as another important appointment. Then on the day when you try to attend the interview, your alarm clock fails to ring and you run late. And on the way to the interview the heal of your shoe breaks.

Stop and pause. Think carefully and intuitively. Is this really the right job for you? The angels are using resistive powers to put obstacles in your way for good reason. If it was the right job, they would have smoothed the way to make it easy for you.

You should change your original request. Instead, you should ask the angels to help you find the right job for you. You can suggest the type of work you want, but try not to be too specific about one job. If you find a job that fits the bill, then go for it, and pay heed to the signs, coincidences and synchronicities to help you decide if it is the right one for you.

Angel Protection

Angels are always ready to protect you. You only have to ask. You can also ask them to protect others.

You may want to ask for protection at the beginning of each day or night.

Simply close your eyes and enter your relaxed state, and say "I ask the angels to protect me as I start this new day."

Or, "I ask the angels to protect my family and keep them safe from harm and free from danger."

If you asking for protection for a planned travel arrangement, then say, "I ask the angels to protect me on my journey today, and that my travels will be harmless and that I will reach my destination safe and sound."

At the end of each request, you should say, "I thank the angels for hearing me."

Angels will always help you, but you must never take them for granted. You should always show gratitude.

The protection you have asked for will last for as long as you have requested it, ie, for the day or until the end of the journey.

If you require immediate protection, you can ask for this too. For example, if your house is on fire and you are in immediate danger, do not hesitate. Ask for protection there and then. They will not ignore you. They will be there.

If you are looking for specific protection, you may choose to ask Archangel Michael, who can protect you from real or imaginary fears, amongst other things.

If you are asking for help from an Archangel, then you must request their presence by name to identify them.

Angel Shielding

In line with protection, angels can shield us from harm when we ask.

When in your relaxed state, just say, "I ask that the angels protect and shield me now, and I thank the angels for hearing me."

The angels will provide a personal shield of protection around you, which will stay in place until you ask for it to be removed.

This shield may also protect you from other people who may want to try to manipulate, wrongly influence, bully or impose on you.

We can often tell when a situation is not right, when something we are being told or asked of makes us feel uneasy or sets alarm bells off in our minds. Immediately ask for protection from the angels.

Shielding from Evil

As we have already discussed, the fallen angels will try to test you, leading you away from your true path towards ruin. If you think you are being tested, or if you feel temptation is drawing you away from what is good, then ask for angel shielding.

When in your relaxed state, say, "I ask that the angels shield me from all evil or bad spirits that I encounter now, in this life or from any past life, and I thank the angels for hearing me."

The angels will hear you and will come to your assistance.

For all types of protection, you must have faith. You will only recognise the help the angels give you when you are spiritually open to receive them. At all times, when you ask, they will come and they will stay until you no longer need them.

Angel cards are classed as a type of oracle card. Oracle cards are those which are used in a clairvoyant or spiritual sense. They are tools with the power to provide insight and guidance. Angel cards will provide messages of guidance, support and comfort.

There are many different types decks of varying sizes of angel cards. When you decide to buy a deck, you can ask the angels to help you choose. Then you must choose the deck that you are most drawn to. This is the right set of cards for you.

When you have your cards, take off the cellophane wrapper and ask the angels to bless them and guide you with them.

Then, taking your time, look through each card, touching each card, attaching your thoughts to them, energising them and getting to know them. Do not let other people touch them. They are yours and must only resonate with your energy vibration.

When you are ready to start using them, ask the angels your request. Then you may choose a one card draw, three card draw or all card draw.

One Card Draw

Shuffle the cards. If a card falls out, then this is the one for you to regard. If not, then randomly select one card. Now regard your card with a relaxed mind and see what message comes to you. Use your intuition. It will answer, guide, support or comfort you, according to your request.

Remember to thank the angels for hearing you when you have finished.

Three Card Draw

Shuffle the cards. Then choose three cards and place them face down. Discard the rest of the deck.

Turn the first one over. This card represents a recent past situation in relation to your current request. It is the background to the present.

Turn the second card over. This card represents the situation as it exists in the present day.

Turn the third card over. This card represents the outcome and how to get there.

Each time you turn over a card, study it. Let your mind relax and wander. Let the images, colours and words seep into your mind and find the true meaning. The angels will use the cards as a channel to communicate and answer your request.

All Card Draw

Shuffle the cards. Then start placing the cards face down in rows of ten.

Turn them over, one by one from the top, and read them however you feel. Think about what each card is saying to you personally. Think about the order of the cards, which cards follow which. Consider any emerging patterns you may notice. Remember, the angels will use these cards as a channel to communicate with you. They will guide you to your answer through your intuitive understanding of the placement of these cards.

Angel altars are not essential for angel communication. Many people like to set them up to enhance and direct their spiritual experience.

An angel altar may be set up indoors at your home or outside in your garden. It is a place where you can focus your connection with the angels.

There is no set example of an angel altar. It should be unique and individual to you.

You can place it anywhere in your home, but it should be in a place that you see every day. It should also be in a quiet space that is calm, peaceful and happy.

Choose a flat space and lay out a cloth on it. You can lay your altar out in a manner that feels right for you, but many people like to put the largest items at the back. What you place on your altar will also be individual and there is no right or wrong.

Examples of what people place on angel altars are:

- A white cloth
- A silver tray
- Angel related ornaments
- Candles
- Crystals
- Bells
- Angel cards
- Written prayers or affirmations
- Angel books
- Feathers
- Flowers

- Fragrances

Etc etc.

Always try to keep the altar clean and fresh, pretty and bright. Adding crystals and candles to your altar brings a spiritual light and energy and keeping it aesthetically pleasing to your eye will encourage you to feel accomplished and ready to receive a spiritual experience.

Daily Rituals

When you feel comfortable, you can bring angels into your life every day, and your life will change for the better. You will be able to develop an intimate connection with the angels, and in turn, will experience expansion in personal awareness and spiritual growth while you follow the true path of your life.

Morning Ritual

Every morning of your life is different, but you can always spare a few moments to connect with angels. You should start every morning with an angelic ritual.

Take yourself into your relaxed state. Say thank you to the angels who have protected you during the night while you slept.

Acknowledge and be grateful for the new day.

Ask the angels to show you what you need to know for the day.

Ask that they stay at your side during the day.

Ask for any specific help that you will require upon this day, whether it be to find a new job, a new love, or inner peace. Now is the time to request it.

Thank the angels for hearing you.

You are now ready to embrace the day with the knowledge that the angels are with you, guiding and supporting you, and available to offer you further assistance should you ask. Be watchful for signs, coincidences and synchronicities. The angels will be guiding you, leading you along the correct path of your life.

Evening Ritual

Every evening, last thing before you settle to sleep, partake in this ritual to reflect on the day.

If you have an altar, sit by it, light a candle and take yourself into your relaxed state.

Tell the angels of any signs you had noticed during the day, acknowledging their connection.

Thank the angels for staying by your side.

Ask them to visit you in your dreams.

Ask that they stay and protect you and your family overnight and protect your home from harm.

Thank the angels for hearing you.

These daily rituals are merely examples. You can adjust them to suit your own feelings. And they can change from day to day. They can be short and simple, or longer and more complex in detail.

The purpose of these daily rituals will be unique to you, to raise your inner awareness, or to bring about a sense of calm, or to enable and develop your journey on the spiritual path of your life.

As with all divine angelic connections, each communication is special and sacred and should be honoured as such. Practicing gratitude and respect of the angel world allows you to continue to align and focus your spiritual beliefs.

Your guardian angel, the legions of regular angels and the Archangels are there for you, at any time. You are unique and loved. Their mission is to lead you along the spiritual path towards enlightenment. Their desire is to assist, guide, support, protect, comfort and help you in any way that you request for the good of yourself and others.

You will always have free will. It is always your choice. Choose to listen to the communications from angels and follow your true life's path.

All you have to do is have faith and ask!

End

Index

References

Acone S. (2018) Healing Crystals, www.healingcrystals.com

Alexander, H (2002), The Practice of Daily Rituals, www.holisticshop.co.uk

Amorth, G (2016) An Exorcist Explains the Demonic: The Antics of Satan and His Army of Fallen Angels, New Hampshire , Sophia Institute Press

Angel, (2015) What Are Angel Cards and How To Read Them, www.wishingmoon.com

Angel Therapy, Encyclopedia of Occultism and Parapsychology (2019) Encyclopedia.com

Aquinas, T. (1270) Summa Theologica, 5 Vols

Archangel Correspondences (2018) www.archangels-and-angels.com

Baines, W. (nd) The Spheres of the Christian Angelic Hierarchy, www.beliefnet.com

Beauregard, M., O'Leary, D. (2009) The Spiritual Brain, New York, Harper Collins

Beckler, M. (2014) Seven Archangels – Understanding the 7 Angels of the Week! www.ask-angels.com

Beckler, M (2014) Understanding Crystal, Rainbow and Indigo Star Children, www.ask-angels.com

Beckman-Murray, R., Proctor-Zenter, J. (1989) Nursing Concepts for Health Promotion, London, Prentice-Hall

Brewer, D. (2019) Sacred Geometry Book of History, Meanings and How To Create Them, Lulu Press

Castro, R. (2017) Hierarchy of Heaven, www.medium.com

Corrigan, K., Michael-Harrington, L. (2014) Pseudo-Dionysius the Areopagite, www.plato.stanford.edu

Dao, J. (2011) Children of the Stars – Indigo, Crystal and Rainbow Children, www.thepyramidoflight.com

Davies, J. (2017) What is Clairaudience and How To Find If You Possess this Rare Ability, www.learning-mind.com

Demers, D (nd) The 7 Archangels and Their Meanings, www.beliefnet.com

English Oxford Living Dictionaries, (2019) www.en.oxforddictionaries.com Oxford University Press

Hazel, D. (2019) Angels in the Tarot Cards, wwwbiddytarot.com

Eichler, A. (2011) Animism is Actually Pretty Reasonable, www.theatlantic.com

Estrada, J. (2018) What The Heck Is An Aura, and What Do All The Pretty Colours Mean? www.wellandgood.com

Eugene (2018) Archangels, & Angel Numbers, www.thesecretofthetarot.com

Foor, D. (2017) Animism and Earth Ritual, www.ancestralmedecine.org

Got Questions Ministries, What is Animism? (2019) www.gotquestions.org

Guiley, R. E. (1996) Encyclopedia of Angels, Facts on File

Hazel, D. (2019) Angels in the Tarot Cards, wwwbiddytarot.com

James, W. (1914) The Energies of Men, New York, Moffat, Yard and Co.

Krentzman, A. R. (2016) Taking Charge of your Health and Wellbeing, www.takingcharge.csh.umn.edu/what-spirituality

Lee, J. (2019) Clairvoyance – Everything a Newbie should Know, www.intuitivesouls.com

Lee, J. (2012) What is a Clairvoyant, www.psychic-readings-guide.com

Marquis, N. E. (nd) The Eight Clair Senses, www.wisdomwithin.co

Melchizedek, D. (2000) The Ancient Secret of the Flower of Life, Volume 2, Flagstaff, Light Technology Publishing

Newcomb, J (2019) How To Create An Angel Altar At Home, www.soulandspiritmagazine.com

Padre (2018) 12 Signs of Angels Which Means Your Angels are Near You! www.guardian-angel-reading.com

Pavlina, E. (2010) How To Develop Cognizance, www.erinpavlina.com

Peck, J. A.(2014) The Nine Ranks of Angels, www.preachersinstitute.com

PersianDNA (2007) Angels in Zoroastrianism, www.persiandna.com

Puchalski, C., Ferrell, B., Virani, R., Otis-Green, S. (2009) Improving the Quality of Spiritual Care as a Dimension of Palliative Care: The Report of the Consensus Conference. Journal of Palliative Medecine. Washington Institute for Spirituality and Health

Rodick, E (2017) What are the Names of the Seven Archangels with a Scriptural Support?, www.quora.com

Russell, M (2014) Your Spirit Guardians – The Archangels, www.witchofwalkerville.com

Schultz, K. L. (2011) Zener Cards – Testing ESP, www.esp-realm.blogspot.com

Smith, S (2018) The Forgotten Clairs – Clairgustance and Clairalience, www.annasayce.com

Susan, (2019), Demon-Daimon-Daemon – Greek Word of the Day Lost in Translation, www.greekerthanthegreeks

Tooley, A. (1997) Sacred Geometry, www.energyandvibration.com

Vocabulary.com Dictionary (nd) www.vocabulary.com

White, L (nd) 6 Signs You Are Being Visited By Your Guardian Angel, www.beliefbnet.com

Also by Debbie Brewer

If you enjoyed this book, you may also enjoy:

Sacred Geometry, Book of History, Meanings and How To Create Them

Written By Debbie Brewer

Why is it that we are so drawn to and enticed by sacred geometry? They start with simple mathematical shapes, that combine to create elaborate illustrations of such

beauty and elegance that we marvel at them. Beliefs, religious, spiritual and cultural, have been historically attached to them. The specific design and creation of each individual sacred geometric pattern is thought, among many cultures, not only to demonstrate an understanding of specific universal concepts, but to hold powers of mystical possibilities. The aim of this book is to provide an understanding of the history, creation and meanings of sacred geometry for those who are new to the subject, and to open an insight into the beliefs placed upon them with the hope that it will inspire the reader's interest and imagination and increase their enthusiasm. Enjoy learning how such simple shapes can evolve into inspiring and powerful patterns that weave through the fabric of our entire universe and reality.

Available through all usual book channels.

Connect with the author

www.facebook.com/DebbieBrewerPoetry

www.instagram.com/poetrytreasures

www.twitter.com/poetrytreasure

www.debbiebrewerauthor.com